How to Grow
ORCHIDS

By the SUNSET Editorial Staff

Lane Books • Menlo Park, California

FOREWORD

For too many years the public image of orchids has been that of supremely beautiful flowers produced from plants that require highly specialized and costly growing arrangements to survive, let alone to grow well. While casting a rather fascinating aura of mystery over these plants, this image did them a great disservice—denying their beauty to the many people who would have liked to try growing orchids but assumed they lacked the proper skills and equipment.

In this book we have tried to dispel this mystery and thereby open the door to the beautiful world of orchids so that you can include the enjoyment of their varied charms in your daily living. Whether indoors at windows, outdoors for patio decoration, for greenhouse growing, or as corsages and cut flowers, there are orchids that will give you great satisfaction for only a small outlay of care.

We wish to extend special thanks to the American Orchid Society, to Armacost & Royston Orchids, Inc., and to Hausermann's Orchids, Inc., for making photographs available to us, to Shaffer's Tropical Gardens, Inc., and to Rod McLellan's Orchids for allowing photographs to be taken at their grounds.

Researched and written by Jack Kramer

Edited by Philip Edinger

PHOTOGRAPHERS

ANDREW R. ADDKISON: 12 (top right), 15 (bottom), 30 (top), 33, 34 (top), 36 (top), 37, 39 (top right). AMERICAN ORCHID SOCIETY: 6 (courtesy of R. I. M. Campbell), 9 (all), 17, 23 (bottom), 30 (bottom left), 36 (bottom), 51 (top left and right, 55 (top). WILLIAM APLIN: 42 (top). ARMACOST & ROYSTON, INC.: 55 (bottom), 59. B & G INTERNATIONAL PHOTOS: 46 (top left). NANCY BANNICK: 20 (right). LORRAINE MARSHALL BURGESS: 63 (bottom left). GLENN CHRISTIANSEN: 49 (bottom right). ROBERT COX: 8 (bottom), 25 (bottom). GORDON W. DILLON: 7 (bottom right). G. & S. LABORATORY: 52. LORD & BURNHAM: 27 (bottom). ROD McLELLAN CO.: 15 (top). JACK McDOWELL: 12 (bottom right), 23 (top), 50 (bottom), 53 (bottom). ELLS MARUGG: 18 (all), 19 (all), 41, 45 (all), 51 (bottom), 60 (bottom). DON NORMARK: 26, 27 (top). DARROW M. WATT: 4, 7 (top, bottom left), 10, 12 (left), 16 (bottom), 29, 30 (bottom right), 34 (bottom right), 39 (top left), 42 (bottom left and right), 44, 47, 50 (top), 60 (top), 61 (all), 62, 63 (bottom right). R. WENKAM: 16 (top), 20 (left), 21 (bottom), 53 (top). JOYCE R. WILSON: 11 (all), 21 (top), 25 (top), 28, 32, 34 (bottom left), 39 (bottom), 56 (all), 57 (all). GEORGE WOO: 49 (top left and right, bottom left).

FRONT COVER: Laeliocattleya hybrid Copperglen; photograph by Joyce R. Wilson.

BACK COVER: photograph by William D. Carter

INSIDE FRONT COVER: *Rhyncostylis gigantea,* cymbidium hybrid, and cattleya hybrid photos by Joyce R. Wilson; *Dendrobium moschatum* photo by Andrew R. Addkison; miltonia hybrid photo by Hermann Pigors.

INSIDE BACK COVER: *Laelia superbiens* and *Odontoglossum grande* photos by Andrew R. Addkison; miltonia hybrid and paphiopedilum hybrid photos by Hermann Pigors; *Paphiopedilum fairieanum* photo by Joyce R. Wilson.

Executive Editor, Sunset Books: David E. Clark

Eighth Printing January 1975

CONTENTS

Special Features

*TWO MEMBERS
of the fascinating and
highly variable orchid family:
At the left is a
phalaenopsis hybrid, while
the plant at the right
is a hybrid paphiopedilum.*

Presenting the Orchids

A diversified family with universal appeal

THOSE colorful, enticing orchids that look so beautiful in corsages from the florist are not only to be admired on special occasions. The familiar gift orchids and many, many more can be easily grown at home without special equipment or elaborate care. Because of improvements in cultural and propagating techniques, they are no longer expensive; a mature plant with four or five flowers may cost less than ten dollars; younger and smaller plants will be much less.

While the most familiar orchids (the usual corsage types) are cattleya, cymbidium, and paphiopedilum species and hybrids, there are also numberless intriguing and attractive species from all parts of the world from which to choose to decorate your home. You will find orchid flowers in all colors except true black, the predominant shades being lavender, pink, rose, red, yellow, and white. Frequently two or more colors, often contrasting, will appear in a single flower.

Orchid blossoms range from nearly pinhead size to flamboyant kinds as large as salad plates, many of them providing delightful fragrance in addition to rare beauty. Flowering seasons vary enough so that by selecting according to season of bloom you can have color indoors all year from perhaps only a dozen plants.

The Greeks Had a Word for It

Although the cultivation of orchids has been a relatively recent undertaking, the knowledge and folklore of these plants trace back many centuries to the Orient and to ancient Greece. Confucius mentioned orchids as being flowers of great refinement to be held in high esteem, and it was the Greek philosopher Theophrastus, in the era of Plato and Aristotle, who first called them by the name *orchis* from which the word "orchid" is derived. From Grecian times through approximately the eighteenth century, the native European orchids constituted a part of the herbalists' bag of remedies. The orchid root supposedly was an aphrodisiac and also useful in obtaining a child of whichever sex one desired.

It remained, however, for the plant explorers of the late 1700's to spark an interest in growing orchids purely for ornamental purposes. Expeditions into tropical areas of Mexico, Central America and South America revealed much new material for plantsmen throughout the world.

From Jungle to Greenhouse

While it is true that tropical climates are generally mild and humid, there still exist, within the tropics, sharp distinctions between *how* mild and *how* humid. Plants taken from mountainous regions may be accustomed to definite seasonal fluctuations in rainfall and temperature and to somewhat lower temperatures generally than are plants which grow in lowlands or along rivers. Even though the traveler to the tropics may consider the entire area "hot," the plant species there have distributed themselves according to these various nuances of heat and moisture. Therefore, to know that an orchid comes from Costa Rica is of little value in trying to duplicate native conditions in the greenhouse. To know that an orchid is found along watercourses in the lowlands is considerably more helpful, yet even within a given location the orchids which grow in treetops will prefer more light, air circulation, and lower humidity than will those found growing close to the jungle floor.

Early orchid growers erred on the side of generalization, assuming all native habitats to be hot and steaming. As a result, collected orchid plants, upon reaching European growers, were subjected to artificial greenhouse climates which were more likely to assure their failure rather than success.

Of little help to growers who were trying to solve the "mysteries" of orchid culture were some of the plant explorers and collectors. Because it was the explorer-collector who was able to supply growers with orchid plants from the tropics, collectors who had found especially desirable species often realized the advantage in keeping the location of those plants secret, even to the point of falsifying information to deliberately lead other explorers astray. By so doing, the individual collector could ask high prices for his fine plants because they were an exclusive offering.

Inasmuch as successful orchid culture was achieved only after years of trial and error, many growers found themselves reluctant to divulge *their* secrets lest other growers, both amateur and professional, find orchid growing so easy as to destroy a commercial advantage.

Born from avarice and ignorance, the myth of "difficult" orchids persisted into the twentieth century.

WILD TROPICAL ORCHIDS often seek the treetops and branches for light and fresh air.

GROUP PORTRAIT of popular
orchids includes cattleya
(left), phalaenopsis (upper right),
paphiopedilum and miltonia
(lower right).

FOUR ORCHID GENERA are represented in photo at left: laelia (upper left), odontoglossum (upper
right), miltonia (lower left), and paphiopedilum. Photo at right is Paphiopedilum insigne.

THICK CLUSTERS of white dendrobiums droop gracefully from tree fern trunks which provide foothold for orchid roots.

HYBRID VANDA needs much light. Most Hawaiian orchid leis are made from these flowers.

Distribution In Nature

Popular opinion—abetted by romanticized stories of tropical adventure—placed most orchids as growing naturally in oppressively hot, steaming jungles. A more realistic look at the orchid family will reveal that a number of species flourish in the warm temperate regions throughout the world. A few representatives can be found even in such unexpected places as frigid mountain areas or in deserts, or as near-aquatics in streams. Pleione species, for example, often break through snow to flower, while a few rare Australian species are actually subterranean—only barely reaching the soil surface at flowering time. The west coast of South America—Chile, Peru, Ecuador, and Colombia—harbors a wealth of native orchids. There they are found in quite mountainous territory where at 6,000 feet above sea level the nighttime temperature average is around 48°.

Perhaps the greatest number of orchid species is found in New Guinea, but Asia, Africa, Borneo, and Central America also have vast regions populated with orchids. Ironically, although Hawaii abounds with orchids, only three insignificant kinds are native; all the showy sorts have been planted there by man.

ORANGE-YELLOW FLOWERS and abundant leaves nearly obscure the container in this specimen of Dendrobium jenkinsii.

Growth Habits

Many of the tropical orchids discovered and collected in the eighteenth and nineteenth centuries were found growing on the trunks or branches of trees. This growth situation spawned the erroneous but persistent belief that orchids were parasites. Actually these plants utilize the trees only for support, receiving their nutrients from whatever the rain washes their way, from bird droppings, and from organic debris that may collect around their roots. Such plants are called epiphytes.

For convenience, orchids may be considered to be of two basic growth habits: epiphytic, as just explained, or terrestrial. The terrestrial species grow with their roots in soil.

Variations on this general theme do occur. There are also orchids that cling to rocks for a foothold; these are generally treated as epiphytes since they usually depend upon natural forces to carry nutrients to them. Some species cannot be absolutely classed as either epiphytic or terrestrial. There are those which begin life growing in soil but which become vine-like and cling to tree-trunks or other convenient supports; then, in later life the soil-rooted part dies away, leaving

MOTH ORCHID HYBRID has delicate veining and dotting on petals and sepals and in the throat.

ORCHID FLOWER STRUCTURE: 1, sepals; 2, petals; 3, labellum (lip); (4), column (under folds of lip).

one growth season; the next year's growth comes from the base of usually the youngest growth. Sympodial orchids may bloom either from the tips of their most recent growth or from the sides or bases of it. Many sympodial orchids form *pseudobulbs*; these are thickened stems which serve as storage for food and water, making it possible for the plants to survive seasons of drought. Leaves may grow along the pseudobulbs or from their tips.

Foliage

Orchid foliage is usually tough and leathery, and succulent in texture as in the popular cattleyas, although occasionally it will be thin and papery as in various sobralias and galeandras. Some species, like *Dendrobium nobile* and *D. superbum*, lose their leaves after growth matures, but the vast majority are evergreen. Some orchids will be handsome foliage plants with masses of dark green leaves (cymbidiums are a familiar example); most species, however, are of limited attractiveness when out of bloom.

Flowers

Despite the outward complexity and variety of orchid flowers, their basic structure is simple. Three *sepals* and three *petals* constitute an orchid flower; the showiest aspect of many orchids—the often-colorful lip—is simply a highly modified petal. Often hidden by part of the lip is a column which contains the reproductive organs.

Flowers are produced in several ways. Many species have pendant blossoms on long spikes, while some may have a solitary flower at the end of an erect stem. Still others are borne along upright stalks that may carry up to a hundred blooms altogether, or are carried in various numbers on upright, branching stems.

Many orchid flowers are true mimics. Some masdevellias look like small kites; catasetums resemble birds in flight; *Anguloa cliftoni* imitates a tulip, while a miniature daisy appearance is given by *Coelogyne ocellata*. Such descriptive names as dove-orchid (*Peristeria elata*), spider-orchid (*Brassia caudata*), and moth-orchid (*Phalaenopsis amabilis*) give some idea of the variety of imitative forms these flowers may take.

the plant a true epiphyte. You will also find some species growing equally happily in trees and in the soil below, where pieces of aerial plants have fallen and taken root.

It is important to know the basic growth habits of the orchids in your possession, for their needs differ correspondingly. Most terrestrials need water throughout the year; most epiphytes must be kept dry during some period of their growth cycle, usually either before or after flowering or at both times.

The Plant

Orchid plants, as they grow and enlarge from year to year, do so generally in one of two ways. Those with a *monopodial* style of growth become taller each year, the result of new growth only at the tip of the stem. Leaves are in two rows on opposite sides of the stem, the individual leaves alternating with those in the opposite row as they climb the stem. Flower spikes and aerial roots will arise from the juncture of leaf with stem or on the stem opposite a leaf.

The second basic growth style—and by far the most prevalent—is *sympodial*. Here, the upward growth of the plant stops, in most cases, after

SYMPODIAL GROWTH is typical of the majority of orchids. New growth originates from base of the youngest plants, matures in one season, produces flowers and then more new growth.

MONOPODIAL GROWTH is exhibited in this plant. New growth is only in an upward direction; aerial roots and flower stalks arise from the central stem.

FROM ASIAN TROPICS at high, cool elevations comes white and yellow Coelogyne cristata.

INTERGENERIC HYBRID between laelia and cattleya, this shows influence of parent Laelia albida.

DELICATE FLOWERS of Epidendrum atropurpureum are combination of chocolate, rose, and green.

UNDERSTANDING ORCHID NAMES

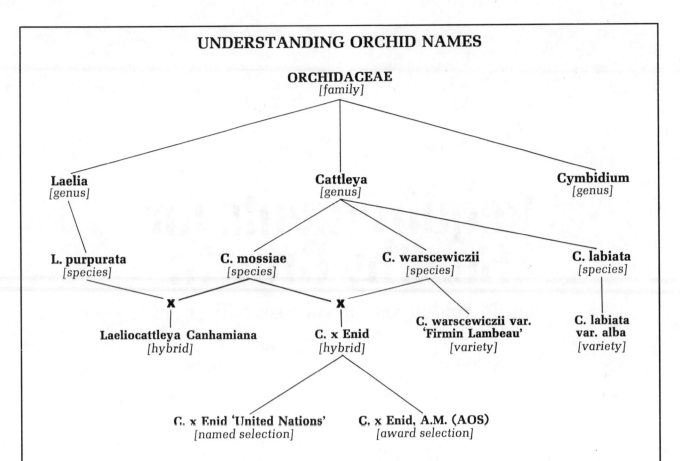

The orchid *family* has been organized by botanists into a number of *genera*, each of which (called a *genus*) contains from one to many *species* which show a close relationship to one another. Thus, the orchids *Laelia anceps* and *Laelia purpurata* are distinct species but with enough characteristics in common to be included in the same genus, *Laelia.*

When two orchid species are crossed, the hybridizer gives that cross a name which all seedlings from that cross are entitled to bear, regardless of who else might make the same cross or how many years later he might make it. For example, all hybrids of *Cattleya mossiae* x *Cattleya warscewiczii* are identified as Cattleya x Enid; the "x" preceding Enid indicates that the plant so named is a hybrid.

Because plants from the same parents will all differ from one another to some extent, the hybrid name is not a guarantee of quality but only of ancestry. Really fine hybrid plants will be further designated in one of two ways: The hybrid name will be followed by another name enclosed in single quotation marks (e.g. Cattleya x Enid 'United Nations') or, if a hybrid has received an award, the award initials following the hybrid name will designate this superior plant.

Within the orchid family, members of different genera can often cross with greater ease than is possible in other plant families. As a result, a number of intergeneric hybrids have been produced. To designate these hybrids, the genus name is replaced by a name coined from those of the genera which produced the hybrid. Laeliocattleya x Mrs. J. Leeman, therefore, is a hybrid between a laelia species and a species of cattleya. In some cases where so many genera are involved in a hybrid's background that the coined name becomes unmanageable, a set of "code names" has been internationally established to indicate hybrids of particular intergeneric backgrounds. *Potinara* is the coined "genus name" for hybrids involving brassavola, cattleya, laelia, and sophronitis, although jawbreakers like *Dialaeliocattleya* still exist.

Any species will exhibit some variation from plant to plant in the wild, so it is natural that orchid growers should want to propagate an especially good representative of unexpected color variation of a species. The abbreviation "var.", for "variety," indicates a selected form.

Requirements for Healthy Growth

Simple guidelines for success with orchids

THERE are no longer any secrets about orchid growing, but there are some general rules to follow which, combined with common sense, can turn a brown thumb green. By their appearance and performance the orchid plants themselves will indicate their needs; it is up to you to recognize these signals from the plants and to understand their requirements.

TEMPERATURE AND HUMIDITY

Orchids may be conveniently grouped into general categories according to the temperatures they prefer for their best growth. Average winter home temperatures of 56° to 62° at night and 62° to 80° during the day will suit a great number of different plants. Those that prefer cool conditions—odontoglossums, miltonias, masdevallias, and maxillarias, for example—will be happier in temperatures that range about 10 degrees less than those just listed. On the other hand are orchids like dendrobiums, oncidiums, epidendrums, and cattleyas that need temperatures about 10 degrees warmer.

Fortunately, this does not mean that you must have separate rooms for those that prefer cool or warm temperatures. It is an easy matter to place some plants closer to the window where the temperature will be lower in winter; positions farther from the window pane will likely suit those that require more warmth.

Summer temperatures are frequently high, but a few days of excessive heat may not harm plants. If there is a long warm spell, try to keep plants as cool as possible. Outdoors, natural air currents constantly cool plants; in confined indoor areas excessive heat can be more harmful, especially if ventilation is poor.

You need not turn your home into a steaming jungle for your orchids. Most of these plants respond admirably when the amount of moisture in the air (humidity) is between 30 and 40 per cent—which is a healthy figure for people, too. A few species do need excessive humidity (as high as 80 per cent), but these are the exceptions rather than the rule. As temperatures lower in the evening, so should the humidity as a precaution against the disease organisms which thrive in cool temperatures and moisture (see page 22). To measure humidity in a room, buy an inexpensive *hygrometer* (available from many hardware dealers).

Humidity is always easier to raise than it is to

AMPLE LIGHT AND HUMIDITY are provided by a window location and a tray of moist gravel from which water can evaporate.

lower. Gravel-filled trays which catch excess water from routine waterings will provide some humidity increase as the water evaporates from the surface of the stones. Misting the air around plants with a spray gun also increases humidity as does the time-tested method of placing pans of water near radiators. During spring and summer you should mist orchids daily; decrease the frequency in autumn and winter.

A number of mist guns suitable for this purpose are available, but whether you use a window-cleanser bottle or an expensive sprayer you should never mist plants directly at close range. Instead, spray the area around the plants so that some moisture settles on the foliage but will evaporate by evening. You run the risk of diseased plants if water remains overnight on foliage or in crowns of plants (see page 22). If you have many plants growing together, the plants themselves will create additional humidity by their natural transpiration.

Many furnace systems in newer homes are equipped with humidifiers. Where no such equipment exists, you can buy space humidifiers that will sufficiently increase humidity for a room. These usually consist of a small motor-driven fan that breaks up water droplets into a fine mist.

HUMIDITY IS INCREASED automatically whenever a number of plants are grown together.

GOOD AIR CIRCULATION and easy watering are achieved by hanging pots of phalaenopsis plants.

PLASTIC CONTAINER is lightweight, easy to clean for re-use, good for plants grown in fir bark.

LIGHT AND VENTILATION

In nature, orchids seldom grow in complete shade nor where air is stagnant. Instead, they thrive in dappled sunlight and where there is a free circulation of air. A "fresh" atmosphere is essential if you want healthy flowering plants.

Air circulation in the home is generally satisfactory during summer because some windows are almost always open. In winter, however, if you cannot keep a window slightly ajar, use a small oscillating fan to keep air moving. Do not direct the fan at the plants, as they will not tolerate drafts; instead, position the fan so that the flow of air is directed above or below your orchids.

While there are many orchids that will thrive at a sunny window, the sun and light requirements do vary considerably among the various species and hybrids. Therefore, it is vital that you select plants which will perform best under the conditions you can provide. Do not, for example, place a sun-loving orchid in a shady location: It will not bloom. Conversely, a shade-loving plant grown in a sunny spot will likely develop leaf scorch. In both cases disappointment will result from unsatisfactory performance. Sometimes moving a plant only an inch or two—into more or less sun than it had been receiving—will make the difference between a really healthy plant and one that simply exists.

CONTAINER CULTURE

Throughout years of cultural experimentation, orchids have been grown in everything from coconut shreddings to charcoal and gravel. An ideal medium for all plants is difficult to find, as each medium has its inherent advantages and disadvantages. Fir bark is now the most popular orchid potting material in most regions; osmunda (the traditional medium) is still frequently used with great success but with less ease.

Fir bark is sold as chunks of bark which first have been graded according to size and then steamed to remove any toxic materials which may be present. If you use fir bark for potting your orchids, sift out small particles that are sometimes mixed in during processing; if they remain they may impede drainage. The smallest grades are used for seedlings and miniature plants, medium grades for plants to 30 inches tall, and largest grades for larger plants like vandas and some brassias that prefer a very open growing medium.

Since fir bark contains virtually no nutrients, you may want to use a very weak solution of a commercial plant food every other watering during a plant's growing season. Fertilizers especially prepared for orchids are the simplest to use. In autumn and winter, fertilizing is usually unnecessary for most sorts; only those making new growth during these months will require it.

Bark is easy to work with and can be used wet or dry when potting plants, unlike osmunda which must be pre-moistened before use. Bark is also the best medium for getting roots growing quickly. Because fir bark deteriorates within a year or two, your plants will need to be repotted in fresh bark when this happens. Otherwise, much of the aeration and rapid drainage is sacrificed—to the detriment of the orchid roots.

Osmunda fiber is simply the aerial roots from two types of osmunda fern. The fiber holds water well, drying out slowly over a long period of time, and has spaces between the fibers to permit free circulation of air and drainage of excess water. Osmunda also contains more nutrients than does fir bark, so that plants in osmunda will require less additional feeding than will plants in bark. Usually within two to three years osmunda decays and must be replaced. So that it will be easy to handle when you pot your orchids in it, first soak osmunda overnight in water.

Terrestrial and semiterrestrial orchids like calanthe, pleione, and some paphiopedilums are best grown in a medium which consists of entirely organic materials. Chopped osmunda, leaf mold, and small grade fir bark (without removal of fine particles) in equal parts form a mixture that is generally satisfactory. A few orchids will even thrive in garden soil (see Chapter 4).

Containers

Orchids can be grown in any kind of container which has a hole for drainage in its base. Because ventilation around the bottom of the pot is vital to an orchid plant's well-being, excess water must not accumulate at the roots. For these reasons, slotted clay pots are made specifically for orchids; these are first-choice containers for your plants. If you use a standard clay pot (without the slotted base), enlarge the drainage hole by gently chipping away its edges.

A redwood basket with spaces between the laths is an ideal container for many species, especially plants of stanhopea, acineta, and gongora which produce flower spikes that grow almost straight downward from the base of the plant. A wire basket, although perhaps not as pleasing esthetically, is another good choice for many orchids.

Plastic or glazed ceramic containers will hold moisture over a much longer period of time than will clay pots or baskets. Consequently you will have to guard against overwatering orchids grown in the non-porous containers. Fir bark, because it dries more rapidly than does osmunda, is a better planting medium for orchids in plastic or glazed ceramic pots.

Some epiphytic orchids don't even need a container in which to grow. Miniatures and smaller species are often grown successfully on rafts or slabs of osmunda or tree fern fiber, or on pieces of bark or logs. These slabs may be suspended from ceiling hooks or hung on walls—duplicating an aerial environment from the wild.

SPECIALLY MADE for orchids, this clay pot has enlarged, slotted drainage holes.

1. *Cattleya orchid ready for repotting: Youngest rhizomes are growing over the pot's edge.*

2. *Remove as much of old potting mixture as you can from roots; fingers are best tools.*

Potting Procedures

Orchids growing in 5, 6, 7, or 8-inch containers usually need repotting every eighteen months. By this time, those with a sympodial growth habit (see page 10) will have begun to overgrow their containers and the bark or osmunda may have started to break down and lose its open texture. Larger plants (in larger containers) should not be disturbed for several years or until the potting material starts to lose its texture.

Your first consideration in potting orchids is to be sure that containers are absolutely clean. Clay pots and the broken pieces of pots used for drainage should be scrubbed in scalding water before use.

Removing a plant from its old container should be done with care: Live roots may be damaged if you attempt to pull out or force the plant. Gently tap the outside of the pot with a hammer, or strike the pot's edge against a table top; this should free the root ball from the container. Gradually jiggle the plant out of its old potting mix, then crumble off the old mix with your fingers. Examine the root system of all plants and trim dead roots back to living tissue.

Potting in bark. Fill the bottom one-third of the container with pieces of broken pots, and set the plant in place. Then, fill in and around the roots with fresh bark, occasionally pressing down the potting medium with a blunt-edged stick. Work from the sides of the pot to the center until you have filled the pot to within a half-inch of its rim. If necessary, stake the plant to hold it upright.

Potting in osmunda. Beginning the day before you plan to pot your orchids, soak the osmunda so it will be easy to handle. After it has soaked overnight, cut the osmunda into 3-inch squares with a sharp knife. Then, just as you would if you were potting in bark, fill the container about one-third full with pieces of broken pots and center the plant in place. Orchids grown in osmunda must have their roots tightly packed in the fiber. Fill in and around the roots with the osmunda, adding the material at the edge of the pot, filling in and around the roots and pushing it down rather hard toward the center of the container. A blunt-edged potting stick will help you compact the osmunda. Continue to add osmunda until no more can be fitted in. Finally, trim away any excess fiber.

3. Trim off all dead roots and cut back partially-dead roots (brown) to live tissue (white).

4. Divide plant if necessary (see page 51); place cut end of division against edge of pot.

5. After positioning plant in pot, fill in and around roots with potting material.

6. Firm the mixture by pressing with fingers or tapping pot, then stake plant to hold upright.

Potting in baskets or on slabs. When preparing baskets to receive orchid plants, line them with a thin layer of osmunda and then set plants in place as you would in an ordinary container. Adequate drainage is no problem in baskets, so you need not add the layer of broken pots before planting. If you plan to grow your orchids on slabs of tree fern, first wrap the roots in balls of osmunda. Tie the root ball to the slab with galvanized wire or string; when roots appear to have securely anchored plant to slab, you may cut away the wire or string.

For all newly-potted plants. After potting, set plants in a warm location (60° to 75°) and out of direct sunlight. Roots of most newly transplanted orchids are not capable of absorbing moisture immediately and may rot with too much water. For at least a week following planting withhold water from the rooting medium; instead, mist its surface and the outside of the pot. Following this initial "dry" period, begin watering sparingly. Resume normal watering only after you see that root or plant growth has started.

POUCHES OF HAPUU (tree fern fiber) hold cattleya plants with roots wrapped in osmunda.

WIRE BASKET lined with osmunda provides good drainage, air circulation for epiphytic orchids.

When to Pot Orchids

Following the blooming season and before new growth breaks is usually a period of from two to six weeks which is the optimum time for repotting. Then, the plants are at their most dormant stage and the necessary root disturbance will be felt the least.

Watering and Fertilizing

There is no single rule which will tell you how often to water your orchids; their need for water depends upon several interacting factors. Knowledge of these, however, will allow you to determine the particular needs of your plants and to make adjustments as conditions change.

The sizes of containers in which your plants grow will determine the relative frequency of waterings needed, regardless of other conditions. Orchids in large pots (from 8 to 12 inches) dry out slowly; plants in smaller pots dry out more rapidly as the container size decreases. Baskets and, of course, slabs require water more often than do containers with solid sides. The type of potting medium also helps determine plants' water requirements; fir bark dries more rapidly than does osmunda.

The amount of artificial heat indoors influences the orchids' demands for water: The more heat used, the more water plants will need. Even the weather outdoors exerts an influence. On cloudy days plants cannot use much water because transpiration rates are very low, but on hot sunny days they will need abundant water to replenish that which is lost through the leaves.

A convenient rule-of-thumb would be: When in doubt, don't water. Remember that most orchids have their own water reservoirs, and a few days without moisture will not be harmful. When watering your plants, always use tepid water—about 60°-70°.

Most orchids will tolerate a mild fertilizer (10-10-5) and various frequencies of application. Even so, two general guidelines will help you establish a fertilizing program for your plants. Orchids grown in fir bark will require more nitrogen than will plants in osmunda, and they will need to be fertilized more often. Plants need fertilizer least when they are not actively making new growth and when light intensity is low—during winter months and periods of cloudy weather.

EASIEST and often best solution when repotting overcrowded plant is to break the pot.

FOR EASY WATERING of small plants, dip wire tray of potted orchids into sink filled with water.

PLANT PROBLEMS

SYMPTOM	PROBABLE CAUSE	REMEDY
Leaves turn yellow	Too much sunlight or water	Move plant to a cool place; withhold water for a few weeks
Leaves turn yellow and fall	Natural with many deciduous types	Withhold water; move plant to a cool place to encourage bud formation
Leaves show black or brown areas	Too much sun; or infection by a leaf-spotting disease	Move plant to more shade; or see text for disease control
Limp leaves, soft growth at base of plant	Waterlogged potting mixture	Withhold water; give plant a week with dry potting mix
No apparent sign of new growth	The time is not right, in the plant's growth cycle, for new growth	Keep potting mixture evenly moist; do not force plant with extra feeding or watering
Plant refuses to flower	Proper growth cycle and day-length not being observed	Determine times of year for plant's natural growth and rest periods; keep plant in darkness at night
Buds drop	Temperatures fluctuate too greatly	Move plant to a location having more even temperatures

PLANT PROBLEMS

Many plants, when poorly grown or carelessly handled, will fall easy victim to insects or disease. In this respect orchids are no different. However, with reasonable attention given to their basic needs their troubles will be few.

Your greatest assets in handling plant problems will be a sharp eye for any appearance or performance that seems abnormal. The check list on this page of possible problems will familiarize you with symptoms, causes, and remedies for troubles that arise from unfavorable growing conditions. In the following paragraphs are discussed the more common insect and disease organisms that are known to bother orchids.

Insects, Diseases, and Remedies

If you discover insects in your orchid collection, your first job is to identify them. Chewed leaves may result from the activities of weevils, cattleya flies, sowbugs, springtails, snails, or slugs. Mottled or disfigured foliage usually indicate the presence of a sucking insect: scale, thrips, mealy bugs, or spider mites.

Light infestations of many insects can be removed by hand or brushed away with a solution of detergent and water. Only the microscopic insects (thrips and spider mites) or heavy populations of scale or mealy bugs that have invaded hard-to-reach areas of the plants will require spraying with an insecticide.

Snails and slugs, if not removed by hand, are best controlled by a metaldehyde bait. Diazinon sprays will eradicate the other pests mentioned; a spray containing malathion is satisfactory for these other pests except for spider mites.

Fungus and bacterial diseases are usually noticed as a collapse of the plant's tissues, frequently with a water-soaked appearance. Depending upon the disease, the part of the plant attacked may be leaves, stems, pseudobulbs, or roots.

Diverse as they are, these diseases are alike in requiring a high humidity to thrive. Some appear with humidity and low temperatures while others are not activated until temperatures are relatively high. To discourage disease organisms, water your orchids as early in the day as you can. By the time the temperature has reached its peak the plants will be dry, remaining so as the temperature falls for the night.

Should any plant become diseased despite routine precautions, immediately isolate it from other healthy orchids. Cut out all diseased parts of the plant, then sterilize the cutting tool to prevent its carrying the infection, should you use it again on a healthy plant. Treat the cut surfaces with a fungicide: Natriphene, Bordeaux mixture (copper sulfate and lime), or mercury compounds (highly poisonous) are satisfactory. Decrease water and humidity while the plant is recovering.

Virus infections in orchids may take innumerable forms, but they may generally be recognized by an abnormal patterning in the leaves. This patterning—often in yellow or shades of brown, and sometimes in watery streaks—may be reinforced by flowers which are streaked, malformed, or have colors broken into patches rather than smoothly blended, and which last but a fraction of their normal life.

Unfortunately, there is no cure for virus infections, and plants so affected *must* be destroyed. Insects and cutting tools can spread the virus to other healthy plants in a collection.

BROWN SPOT on leaf usually indicates sun scorch; occasionally it may be evidence of leaf-spot disease.

SEVERE SCALE INFESTATION on leaves and pseudobulbs may be controlled by spraying or wiped off with a detergent and water solution.

Indoors...and Under Glass

At a window, under lights, or in greenhouses, orchids are easy

WHETHER you live in a city apartment or a home in the country, whether you have a greenhouse, a sunny window, or grow plants in a basement under artificial lights, there are many orchids you can grow successfully. If you have limited space for plants, choose from the delightful miniature or dwarf species and hybrids that grow no more than 12 inches tall; if a window sill is your growing area, make your selections from the thousands of medium sized plants that may reach 30 inches. For a special place or for patio decoration, larger plants are available. With some 30,000 species and an equal number of hybrids, there are plants for every place in almost any situation.

ORCHIDS AT YOUR WINDOW

Plants that will not exceed 30 inches in height are the most satisfactory choices for the average window. Six or seven of them, carefully selected, will present a colorful scene almost all year. For your greatest pleasure, avoid those species that have less than attractive growth habits, and always select plants that will adapt themselves to the growing environment you can provide.

In the lycaste, epidendrum, oncidium, and paphiopedilum groups you will find many candidates for window gardens that are neither too large for the space nor culturally demanding. Most important, they may be depended upon to bloom every year; in fact, many of them perform better in the home than in a greenhouse. Unlike many other house plants, orchids rarely attract insects, so it is seldom necessary to use insecticides indoors.

The following orchids rarely grow over 30 inches tall, require little care, and will bloom at an east, west, or south exposure. All of them may be potted in fir bark and will thrive in average home temperatures where humidity is 30 to 40 per cent. For descriptions of these species in more detail, see the lists on pages 31-38, 41-44, and the chapter on favorite orchids, pages 58-63.

Aerides odoratum: white and magenta; summer

Cattleya skinneri: magenta; summer

Coelogyne massangeana: ochre-brown; variable

Epidendrum atropurpureum: brown, green; spring

Epidendrum nemorale: rose-purple; summer

Lycaste aromatica: yellow; winter

VENTILATION AND HUMIDITY are furnished by *wood slats* resting on bed of moist gravel. Plants receive ample light at *window.*

Lycaste deppei: green, white; variable

Odontoglossum grande: brown, yellow; fall

Oncidium ampliatum: bright yellow; spring

Oncidium splendidum: yellow, brown; winter

Paphiopedilum fairieanum: white, green; fall

Paphiopedilum insigne: white, green; winter

Phalaenopsis amabilis: white; winter

Trichopilia suavis: white, pink; spring

The following species can reach 4 feet tall, so are for larger window areas than those in the preceding list. Otherwise, the same cultural guidelines apply.

Aerides multiflorum: white, purple; summer

Cattleya schroederae: rose; spring

Coelogyne pandurata: green; fall

Dendrobium densiflorum: orange-yellow; spring

Dendrobium superbum: lilac-purple; spring

Epidendrum prismatocarpum: yellow; spring

Laelia anceps: rose-violet; winter

Laelia superbiens: lavender, purple; winter

Vanda coerulea: blue; summer, fall

PLANT STANDS with trays of gravel for humidity display orchids at window which has no windowsill.

INTENSE SUNLIGHT and resultant high greenhouse temperatures can be controlled by applying whitewash to glass surface.

SIMPLEST GREENHOUSE is a lean-to attached to another structure. Greenhouse should be placed to receive nearly full sun all day; shades or whitewash can be used to moderate sunlight.

ORCHIDS IN THE GREENHOUSE

While you do not need a greenhouse to grow orchids, a special place for them with controlled conditions is a convenience. The plants growing together increase the humidity, and watering is easy as there is no concern for where excess water will go. The greenhouse may be a simple lean-to structure, a more elaborate separate building, a garden room incorporated into the house, or even a glassed-in enclosure projecting from a window. Many fine greenhouses have been constructed from salvaged materials.

While plentiful light is one of the basic requirements in successful orchid culture, too much light is to be avoided; leaf scorch and desiccation of plants will be the result. Since most greenhouses are all glass, you must control the light with shades or shading compounds (whitewash) on the glass, especially in summer and sometimes in winter in all-year temperate climates. Few orchids will tolerate sun all year.

Excessive humidity must also be guarded against in the greenhouse. Too much moisture in the air coupled with gray days is an invitation for diseases to invade plants. Keep humidity in the growing area between 40 and 60 per cent and be certain that there is *always* good ventilation to provide the all-important air circulation. During hot summer weather when ventilation is especially important, you may need to utilize an evaporative cooler and fan system to keep the air cool and moving. Strive for a "fresh" atmosphere in the greenhouse.

Bottom ventilation will also contribute greatly to the health of your orchids. Greenhouse benches which are constructed from slats with spaces between each will provide for this important air circulation.

There are several heating devices manufactured for greenhouses, and which one you choose depends upon your individual climate. Most greenhouse manufacturers also supply heating systems; study the literature carefully to decide which unit is best for your conditions.

The frequency of watering greenhouse orchids depends upon many interacting factors, and also upon the needs of the particular orchids you grow. Basically, most orchids should be liberally watered in spring and summer and not so much during the rest of the year. Fogging and misting is always beneficial; this can be done several times a day in hot weather to keep plants cool but is needed less during fall and winter.

DOUBLE CHAMBERED GREENHOUSE *separates orchids that require different temperature ranges.*

SIMPLE FLUORESCENT LIGHT arrangement will accommodate one or two plants in unlighted area.

ORCHIDS UNDER ARTIFICIAL LIGHT

Today legions of indoor gardeners grow plants under lights. Otherwise useless spaces in attics, basements, and poorly-lighted rooms have been transformed into lush greeneries by enterprising gardeners who lack the proper window space to grow quantities of plants. If you choose not to make your own artificial light setup, you may choose from various specially manufactured fixtures.

The right kind of artificial light, its duration and intensity, combined with proper cultural steps, can make orchids flourish in any home or apartment. Special fluorescent lamps for growing plants are sold at many hardware stores, and a complete light setup need not cost more than $25.00.

Research has shown that blue and red portions of the light spectrum are the wave lengths most needed by plants for photosynthesis—the manufacture of food by the plants; fluorescent lights provide these wave lengths. In addition, the far-red rays trigger many growth and flowering responses; these are emitted by ordinary incandescent bulbs. Therefore, a combination of fluorescent and incandescent lights is generally used by most gardeners, at a 5 to 1 ratio: 5 watts of fluorescent to 1 watt of incandescent.

Because orchids are basically high light-intensity plants, a minimum of four 40-watt fluorescent tubes and four 8-watt incandescent bulbs is recommended for successful growing. Extended service bulbs are better than standard ones because they produce more far-red rays and last longer than standard bulbs. You can buy fluorescent fixtures that have reflectors and sockets for incandescent bulbs.

Cool white or daylight fluorescent lamps can be used, but for higher light intensities lamps specifically designed for growing plants are available. Once you have decided on your arrangement and the necessary tubes, you may want to call an electrician to assemble the unit.

Using the four-lamp, 40-watt arrangement with incandescent light included, keep light-loving orchids such as epidendrums, cattleyas, and oncidiums as close to the lamps as possible; a distance of 3 inches is entirely satisfactory. Plants that need less light—phalaenopsis, paphiopedilums and coelogynes—should be placed 12 inches below the tubes. With any arrangement, adjusting plants to the light source is easy; with the light source 12 inches above all plants, those needing more light may be placed on platforms or inverted pots to bring them to the required distance.

Generally, 14 hours of artificial light each day throughout the year is an acceptable length to maintain in the beginning. However, some plants will need a longer exposure to light and others will require less to achieve the optimum environment. To determine the most favorable light duration for your various orchids will require some experimentation and careful observation of the results. It takes orchids many months to become accustomed to artificial light, so do not be disheartened if you lose a few plants at the start. Once adjusted, they will grow easily.

Under artificial lights—just as when grown in natural light—orchids require good ventilation, humidity, and proper watering. Although each gardener will eventually work out a cultural program suited to his particular situation, you will find it best to begin by keeping plants at a daytime temperature of 78° to 85° with a drop of 15 degrees at night. Try to provide 40 to 50 per cent humidity in the growing area and *be sure plants receive adequate ventilation.* Overcrowding and a stuffy atmosphere in an artificial light garden will invite disease and disappointment.

MINIATURE ORCHIDS

Limited growing space need not deny you the pleasure of growing a number of orchids in your home. The many miniature species and hybrids need little space to produce their typically beautiful and exotic blossoms. Because they are small, do not think the flowers are insignificant. Some are large and breathtaking; other species may have a series of smaller blooms shaped to form an oval or an ellipse, yet giving the appearance of one flower. For admirers of the minute, there are also species whose flowers must be seen through a magnifying glass for the greatest appreciation of their intricate beauty.

Many miniature orchids adjust slowly to new conditions, and it is not unlikely that you might experience a few losses. It will take about six months before they become really established. Until you see that they are beginning to grow and establish themselves it is best to water them sparingly (about once a week) and keep them at a bright window where temperatures are around 75°.

Because most miniatures come in 1 or 2-inch thumbnail pots of osmunda which dry out rapidly, you must water them daily. For easier growing, put a group that requires the same environment in a large pot to minimize the danger of rapid drying. A number of plants could also be accommodated on a tree fern slab. Wire a patch of osmunda to the slab, and on this cushion fasten the plants. Then prop the slab against a window frame so that it will rest in a deep clay saucer that will catch excess water. Tree fern slabs may also be suspended from the ceiling if beneath them you have a catch basin for excess water, or if you take them down and water the slabs at the sink.

Whenever you grow miniatures together—in a large pot or on tree fern slabs — select species that require similar growing conditions.

Any of these miniature orchid species should be easy to obtain from orchid specialists. Read the genus descriptions on pages 30-38, 41-44, and 58-60 for general cultural guidelines.

Ascocentrum miniatum (see page 31).

Cattleya aclandiae bears olive green, purple-lipped flowers above papery light green leaves.

Cattleya luteola reaches only 6-7 inches tall, with pale yellow flowers and leathery, 2-inch leaves.

Cymbidium hybrids (see pages 41 and 59-60).

Dendrobium aggregatum (see page 33).

Dendrobium linguiforme has buttonlike leaves atop 1-inch, cylindrical pseudobulbs; the white flowers are carried on arching, 4-inch stems.

Epidendrum mariae reaches about 8 inches when in bloom; leaves are leathery, and the green flowers have broad white lips.

Laelia pumila (see page 35).

Odontoglossum pulchellum (see page 36).

Odontoglossum rossii is a winter flowering species. White or blush pink flowers are flushed and spotted with dark brown; each is 2-3 inches across, from 3-5 borne together in each cluster.

Oncidium cheirophorum (see page 37).

Oncidium triquetrum has narrow, 3-5-inch leaves from which arise, in fall, stems of 1-inch green and purple flowers. Each stem may carry up to a dozen blooms.

MINIATURE CYMBIDIUM (top) is smaller in all parts than standard cymbidium hybrid (lower).

BRAZILIAN JUNGLES *have contributed bifrenaria species to orchid collections. This is* B. tyrianthiana, *usually with cream-white and purple flowers.*

TULIP ORCHID, Anguloa clowesii, *is a terrestrial type, bears yellow flowers in summer.*

LONG, CURVED SPURS *characterize starlike white flowers of* Angraecum sesquipedale.

GETTING ACQUAINTED WITH ORCHIDS

On these pages are listed some of the most widely-grown orchids. Each genus will usually contain a number of species and perhaps some named hybrids. General characteristics of the plants are given to help you estimate which plants may be best suited to the space and conditions you have.

The following orchids have been singled out either because they are easy to grow or because they have some outstanding characteristics which make a little extra effort worthwhile. Most of them can be planted in fir bark or osmunda, a few in a soil mixture; this is noted in the descriptions. Unless otherwise stated, you can grow all these orchids in average home temperatures of 75°-80° during the day and 10 to 15 degrees cooler at night.

Aerides. These are epiphytic orchids from tropical Asia, some of which are very tall. Without pseudobulbs, the plants have a central stem with fleshy green leaves. Graceful pendant spikes carry many closely-set, fragrant flowers of waxy texture in summer. Water copiously in spring and summer, not so much the rest of the year. Grow in bright light.

A. crassifolium. Ten inches tall; amethyst-purple flowers.

A. multiflorum. In summer, white and purple, 1-inch flowers are carried in great numbers on stalks longer than the 9-inch, strap-like leaves. Needs sun and even moisture all year.

A. odoratum. To 40 inches; the numerous 1-inch white flowers are blotched with purple. Its spicy fragrance alone would be reason enough to grow this species.

Angraecum. From Asia and Ceylon, there are several fine epiphytic plants in this group for winter color. They have lovely starlike white or greenish white flowers with long curved spurs. Keep moist all year except in fall; then allow plants to dry out between waterings. Grow in bright light.

A. eburneum. To 48 inches, with 8 or more 3-inch waxy greenish white blooms borne alternately on stems longer than the leaves; the monopodial plants may reach 4 feet, with 9-inch arching, strap-shaped leaves.

A. sesquipedale. To 36 inches, bearing fragrant, 6-inch, ivory-white flowers each with a 10-inch spur. Likes coolness (55°) at night.

Anguloa. This remarkable group of terrestrial orchids with large spoon-shaped leaves produces dramatic tulip-like flowers in summer. Plants have pronounced pseudobulbs and prefer coolness—around 50° at night. Protect them from summer sun or the leaves will scorch, but give them some winter light. When growth has matured (generally in December or January) allow them a four or five week dry rest with only occasional misting. Once bud spikes appear at base of the bulbs, you may resume watering.

A. clowesii. To 36 inches; 3-inch brilliant yellow blooms with creamy white lip.

Ascocentrum. This is a small group of generally epiphytic orchids of monopodial growth (see page 10) ranging from southern China, Formosa, and the Philippines, to Java and Borneo. Plants have leathery leaves and short spikes of small flowers, in early spring to summer, often fifty to a stem. Grow in sun and keep evenly moist.

A. ampullaceum. To 10 inches; bright carmine rose, 1-inch flowers appear in spring.

A. miniatum. To 6 inches; flower color may be brilliant yellow-orange, orange, or orange-red; the 1-inch blooms appear during spring or early summer.

Bifrenaria. These Brazilian epiphytes have large showy flowers, angled pseudobulbs, and dark green leathery leaves. Grow in sun or bright light and rest plants without water for about a month after they bloom.

B. harrisoniae. The 3-inch flowers are fleshy, creamy white with reddish purple lip, on a plant to 18 inches tall. Spring blooming.

Brassia. Here is a group of large epiphytic plants found in Mexico south to Brazil and Peru. The leaves are evergreen, arising from plump pseudobulbs. Flower spikes are generally elongated and pendant carrying many fragrant flowers with long slender petals and sepals. These plants are sun lovers, needing warmth (over 60°) and moisture all year.

B. maculata. To 30 inches; known as the spider orchid with bizarre but beautiful whitish green and brown flowers in early summer.

HYBRID DENDROBIUM of the evergreen cane type, this prefers cattleya conditions most of the year.

Coelogyne. A group containing more than 150 species, these epiphytic orchids are widely distributed throughout India, Malaysia, and New Guinea. Their evergreen plants with dark green, spoon shaped leaves are handsome even when not in bloom. Flowers are generally small (about 1 inch across) in shades of brown, cream, beige, or green and are produced from the centers of the youngest growth. Many species bear pendant spikes. Plants prefer a shady location. Excess water left standing among the leaves will cause the buds to rot.

C. cristata. To 24 inches; lovely large white flowers with a yellow-tinted lip. Winter to spring bloom.

C. massangeana. To 48 inches; pendant stems of ochre-brown flowers have a lip that is stained a dark brown. Sometimes blooms twice a year—in spring and in fall.

Cycnoches. These natives of Mexico, Central America, and South America are commonly known as swan orchids because of the graceful curve of one of the flower parts. Plants are epiphytic, with leaves and flower spikes arising from the tops of the pseudobulbs. Leaves are usually deciduous although the time of year for this is variable. After new growth is completed, plants need a definite rest period for several weeks. Grow them in a brightly lighted location. Flowers usually appear in summer.

C. chlorochilon (ventricosum). To 20 inches; the 4-7-inch flowers are chartreuse, each with a white fleshy lip.

C. egertonianum. To 15 inches tall, with small whitish green flowers on long pendant stems.

Cymbidium (See pages 59-60).

Cypripedium (See page 43).

Dendrobium. With over 1,500 species from India, Burma, Ceylon, China, Japan, and Australia, this is one of the largest orchid groups. Five different growth habits, each with somewhat different cultural requirements, are represented in the genus. These are: pseudobulb types, evergreen cane types, deciduous cane types, evergreen phalaenopsis types, and black-haired, short-stemmed species. All are epiphytic.

Pseudobulb dendrobiums. These need abundant watering until leaves mature. Then, to encourage budding, rest the plants for about a month with-

DECIDUOUS CANE-TYPE *dendrobium, D. pierardii, hails from India, where it receives pronounced rest period after growth matures.*

out water. After flowering has finished, allow another complete dry rest for about 8 weeks. Give these plants a sunny place.

D. aggregatum. To 10 inches; small vivid yellow, sweetly scented flowers in spring.

D. chrysotoxum. To 20 inches, with drooping spikes of 2-inch golden yellow flowers in spring. Bloom originates from old as well as new pseudobulbs.

Evergreen cane types. Plants have fleshy leaves and pendant bunches of flowers borne from nodes at the tops of the canes. Water copiously all year except immediately after flowering when a rest period for about a month is necessary. Give the plants plenty of sun. In late fall place them where they will have cool nights (55°) to encourage budding; see that no artificial light reaches plants during this time.

D. dalhousieanum. To 5 feet; in spring it produces 5-inch tawny yellow flowers marked with crimson.

D. densiflorum. To 5 feet; dark yellow flowers appear in spring or summer.

D. thyrsiflorum. To 5 feet; glistening white flow-

ers with an orange lip. This is a stunning plant when flowering in early spring to summer.

Deciduous cane types. This group includes some of the most popular dendrobium species. Flowers appear on nodes along the top of bare canes. In most species, plants are not truly deciduous for they retain some leaves at all times. In summer, these orchids need abundant moisture and warmth, but when foliage is mature (a solitary leaf instead of a pair of leaves) stop watering for about six to eight weeks to encourage formation of flower buds. Move plant to a sunny, cool (45°-50°) place while leaves fall. When flower buds start to show along nodes of canes, move plants back to warmth and resume watering.

D. nobile. To 40 inches; 2-inch white flowers tipped rose-purple have a crimson blotch at throat. Bloom is in winter and spring. This is a variable species with many named varieties.

D. pierardii. To 30 inches; pendant flowering stems with 2-inch blush white or pink blooms appear in spring.

D. superbum. To 5 feet; spectacular spring color comes from pendant, lilac-purple flowers borne on silver canes.

GLISTENING white and orange flowers of Dendrobium thyrsiflorum completely encircle flower spike.

D. wardianum. To 30 inches; pendant, white flowers tipped purple each have a yellow-stained lip. Blooming season is winter and spring.

Evergreen phalaenopsis types. These plants resent fluctuating temperatures and need moisture all year with only a slight reduction of water during the period between maturation of new growth and the formation of flower spikes. The plants also require full sun and ample warmth. These are the most demanding dendrobiums but are well worth the extra effort needed to grow them well.

D. phalaenopsis. To 18 inches; deep rose flowers with magenta lip are shaped much like a typical phalaenopsis bloom. Fall blooming.

Black hairy-stemmed dendrobiums. These have white spring flowers that will last for two months. Plants need even moisture all year, along with full sun and warmth.

D. infundibulum. Grows to 24 inches and has 4-inch white flowers, marked red or yellow on the lip, in spring through summer.

MILTONIA species and a hybrid show flower structure and color arrangement which earned for them the name "pansy orchid." At left is M. spectabilis; the hybrid Hannover is at right.

Epidendrum. From Central America, Mexico, Brazil, and tropical America, these are terrestrial and epiphytic orchids variable in flower form and plant habit. Some have pseudobulbs and need a decided rest after flowering; others have cane growth and require moisture all year. Flowers come in many different colors and plants are generally easy to grow. Most need sun and warmth. See page 43 for descriptions of other epidendrums easily grown outdoors.

E. atropurpureum. To 16 inches with short, globular pseudobulbs; the 3-inch flowers are chocolate brown and pale green with lips of white and rose-purple, from 4-20 on each stem. Spring or early summer is the blooming season. Rest plants after flowering.

E. nemorale. To 16 inches; 4-inch rose and purple flowers are clustered along 2-foot spikes in spring and summer.

E. stamfordianum. To 30 inches; numerous tiny, fragrant yellow and red flowers are produced in spring on spikes that originate from the bases of tall pseudobulbs.

Laelia. Closely related to cattleyas, these epiphytic orchids range from Mexico to South America. Generally, the plants have one or two evergreen leaves at the tops of the pseudobulbs. Flowers resemble cattleyas but are usually smaller and with narrower petals. Culture is similar to that for cattleyas, although they should receive even more sun for best flowering. After flowering and until new growth starts, laelias need very little water; during the rest of the year they should be allowed to dry out between waterings. For descriptions of laelias suitable for growing outdoors, see pages 43-44.

L. gouldiana. To 30 inches when in bloom; the 3-inch, deep rose flowers are produced in winter.

L. pumila. To 10 inches; the solitary rose-purple blooms have yellow-throated purple lips. It flowers in fall.

L. superbiens. To 5 feet when in bloom; a spectacular giant which bears its 6-inch lavender, purple-throated blooms in rounded clusters of 10-20 on stems that can reach 5-6 feet. Flowering season is usually in winter.

Lycaste. These deciduous or semi-deciduous orchids come from Mexico, the West Indies, Central America, and South America, and are usually epiphytic. The long-lasting and freely-produced flowers are predominantly green, although some are pink, white, yellow, or brown. They thrive in a cool location (50°-55° at night, 10 degrees higher during the day) and with good light but not direct sun. Potting mixture should be well-drained and constantly moist except for a period after flowering when water should be reduced to a minimum until new growth appears.

L. aromatica. To 16 inches; short stems from the bases of new pseudobulbs bear many bright yellow, scented flowers in winter.

L. deppei. To 28 inches; green sepals are dotted with rich brown, petals are white, while the lip is yellow. The 4-inch flowers come at various times of the year.

L. skinneri. To 30 inches; large 5-7-inch white or pink blooms with lip spotted rose to red are produced singly on stems in winter.

Miltonia. Native from Costa Rica to Brazil, the epiphytic miltonias are called pansy orchids because they bear flat-faced, open flowers which resemble pansies in shape and markings. They have elongated pseudobulbs with long, graceful, light green leaves that will produce a clump of foliage a foot or more in diameter. Some species prefer coolness, others need warmth. The cool types have white or pink flowers overlaid with magenta, crimson, or yellow. The warm growers bear yellow or white flowers marked purple or brown. In general, conditions which are good for cattleyas (see page 58) will be satisfactory for miltonias; those preferring cooler temperatures should be grown in the cooler range of cattleya temperature tolerance. They require less light than do cattleyas and want no direct sun.

M. flavescens. To 20 inches; yellow flowers, the lip marked yellow or white and blotched with purple. It flowers in summer and prefers warmth.

M. regnelli. To 12 inches; the 3-inch white flowers are marked with rose-purple at the base of petals, the lip is light pink edged white. Stems with 3-5 flowers each are produced in fall.

M. spectabilis. To 20 inches; flowers have large creamy white sepals and petals, and broad rose-purple lip. Blooms come in summer. Native to Brazil and prefers the warmer temperatures.

M. vexillaria. To 20 inches; flowers (to 4 inches across) are usually some shade of pink to red with a darker lip, up to a dozen on each upright stem; foliage is soft grayish green.

Odontoglossum. Delicate colors and ruffled flower parts characterize the blooms of these epiphytic orchids; predominant colors are white, yellow, brown, and pink. Plants generally have flattened pseudobulbs sheathed with small leaves and with two more leaves at the top. Most species prefer very cool conditions, since native habitats are in foggy regions at high altitudes in the Andes Mountains of South America. Night temperatures around 50° and daytime readings in the low to mid-70s are satisfactory; especially in summer keep day temperatures as low as possible—below 80° if you can. Transplant after flowering in fall or in early spring but never in hot summer weather. Plants thrive under crowded conditions, so use relatively small pots for the size of the plant. Odontoglossums appreciate plenty of light (as long as heat is low) but no direct sun and require watering throughout the year.

O. crispum. To 20 inches; flowers are basically white with fringed edges but are frequently flushed pink and dotted with red or brown. Pendant stems usually appear in spring or summer, although season of bloom is variable.

O. grande. To 24 inches; the "tiger orchid" has 6-inch yellow flowers barred with brown, 3-7 on each foot-long stalk. Blooming season is fall.

O. harryanum. To 20 inches; 3-inch wavy chestnut-brown flowers are variously marked with yellow, white, and purple. Flowers appear in summer or early fall.

O. pulchellum. To 10 inches; not especially showy, but the 1-2 inch waxy white flowers in spring have a lily-of-the-valley fragrance.

O. uro-skinneri. To 30 inches; large scapes carry up to twenty 1-inch green and brown flowers with lavender lips. Blooms appear in early spring.

Oncidium. A large group of epiphytic orchids from Mexico, Central America, the West Indies, and parts of Brazil, most of these produce long spikes of beautiful yellow flowers variously marked with brown. Some species have compressed pseudobulbs topped by one or two fleshy leaves, others are almost without bulbs, and still others have pencil-like leaves. Flowers are small and numerous, or large and few—depending on the individual species. Growing conditions for cattleyas (see page 58) are generally satisfactory for oncidiums. Those native to higher and cooler

DELICATELY SCALLOPED FLOWERS give Oncidium ampliatum the look of a yellow confetti shower.

ABUNDANT SPRAYS of 1-inch yellow flowers cover Oncidium sphacelatum in summer.

elevations will prefer temperatures at the lower end of the preferred range. They appreciate considerable sunlight and require a rest period with no water for several weeks following completion of new growth.

O. ampliatum. To 30 inches; a mature plant of the "turtle orchid" (so named because of the shape of its pseudobulbs) may have hundreds of red-spotted yellow flowers to each stem in early spring.

O. cheirophorum. To 6 inches; fragrant, 1/2-inch yellow flowers with green sepals are produced on dense, branched clusters in fall. Two narrow leaves grow from each short, rounded pseudobulb.

O. crispum. To 1-1 1/2 feet; shiny brown 1 1/2-3-inch flowers with yellow and red at base of segments are borne in profusion on arching stems any time throughout the year. Never let plant dry out completely. Grows well in hanging containers.

O. ornithorynchum. To 14 inches, with hundreds of tiny lilac flowers carried in dense, drooping sprays. Flowers are produced in fall or winter.

O. papilio. To 3 feet when in bloom; flowers are 4-5 inches long and 2 1/2 inches across, produced at any time of year on 2-3-foot long stalks which continue to produce buds on old flower stems for several years. The top sepals and petals stand erect, are brown with bands of yellow; lower sepals and petals curve downward around the lip which is yellow, edged brown.

O. sphacelatum. To 3 feet; sprays of over 200 brown-spotted, 1-inch yellow flowers bloom in spring and early summer.

O. splendidum. To 3 feet when in bloom; the 3-inch flowers are profusely produced in winter. Color is yellow-green, barred and spotted with red-brown; the lip is yellow. Each pseudobulb bears only one leaf.

Paphiopedilum (See pages 60-62).

Phalaenopsis (See pages 62-63).

Rhyncostylis. Native to the Philippines and India, these epiphytic orchids have small colorful flowers tightly packed on long pendant stems, giving rise to their common name "foxtail orchid". Foliage is leathery, strap-like, and grows in a fan shape; growth is monopodial. Plants resent being disturbed when replanting is necessary. At that time, try to remove as much old potting mix as you can without removing the plant from its container; then gently fill in around roots with fresh material.

R. gigantea. To 28 inches; pendant "tails" of hundreds of 1-inch, waxy white, red-spotted flowers appear in summer or early fall.

R. retusa. To 12 inches; pendant, 2-foot spikes carry many fragrant white flowers spotted purple, each about 3/4-inch across. Bloom is in summer.

Sobralia. Terrestrial orchids from Central America, these bear large showy, cattleya-like flowers in summer. Plants consist of tall, reed-like stems that have leaves on alternate sides for their entire length. Give them a sunny location and ample moisture all year, especially in early spring, but decrease the amount for a month after each year's new leafy stems are fully developed. Only mature plants will bear flowers, and by that time plants are often 5-6 feet tall. Plant them in a potting mixture suitable for cymbidium (see page 60).

FOXTAIL ORCHID, Rhyncostylis gigantea, *has tight spikes of red-spotted white blooms.*

S. leucoxantha. To 3 feet; the 4-5-inch white flowers are shaded golden yellow, the throat flushed and lined with orange. Flowering is from spring through summer.

S. macrantha. To 7 feet; crimson-purple, fragrant flowers may reach 9 inches across during the spring and summer blooming season.

Stanhopea. Native from Mexico through parts of South America, the epiphytic stanhopeas bear large flowers in lurid color combinations, each of which lasts only a few days. Because flowers appear on pendant scapes that frequently grow down through the potting mix, basket culture is necessary. Plants need some sun and copious water during growth, not so much moisture during the rest of the year, but never let them dry out completely. Most species are highly fragrant. They prefer the same temperature and humidity ranges as do cattleyas (see page 58) but require shade from direct sunlight.

S. wardii. To 20 inches; 4-6-inch waxy yellow, cream, or greenish white flowers are spotted with red or brown. The flowers' shape, and their carriage on pendant stems, give them the look of flying birds with wings raised. Bloom season is fall. Other similar species are *S. oculata* (yellow with purple markings) and *S. tigrina* (yellow, dark red, and purple).

Trichopilia. From Mexico to Brazil come the epiphytic trichopilia species which have large cattleya-like flowers, either solitary or up to four on each stem. Plants have flat, compressed pseudobulbs tipped with a single leaf but form dense clumps. Give trichopilias the same care as you would give oncidiums: much water during the growing season followed by a 2-3 week rest period, a temperature range comfortable for the home, and some sunlight.

T. crispa. To 14 inches; large cherry red, 5-inch flowers with a fluted, red-spotted white lip are produced in spring or summer.

T. suavis. To 10 inches; creamy white 4-6-inch flowers have trumpet-shaped lips of the same color but heavily fluted and spotted with pink. Early spring is the blooming season.

T. tortilis. To 12 inches; narrow, twisted sepals and petals are brownish purple or rosy lavender while the lip is white spotted with red or brown. Flowering may be in spring or fall.

Vanda. Originally from the Philippines, Malaysia, and the Himalayas, these are now grown extensively as a commercial crop in the Hawaiian Islands. Growth habit is monopodial (see page 10) and some types will eventually reach 4 feet or more. Because many aerial roots form along the stems, the top portion of the plant may be cut off and rooted to give you a plant of more manageable size. The old portion of the plant may produce offshoots which can be removed and potted after they form roots.

Vandas may be separated into two leaf types, only one of which is suited to temperate conditions. Those plants with pencil-like leaves (called *terete*) require so much light to flower that they must be grown in full sun. Because they also must have night temperature above 50°, this limits their use to tropical countries or unshaded and well-ventilated greenhouses having tropical temperatures. Vandas with strap-shaped leaves lack the high light requirements and so may be successfully flowered outside of the tropics. Hybrids of the two leaf-types exist (called *semi-terete*), and these also have the exceptionally high light requirement; however, when these hybrids are crossed back to strap-leaf species the resulting hybrids are generally as successful as the original strap-leaf sorts.

All vandas appreciate plenty of water but must have perfect drainage; they enjoy humidity that is somewhat higher than is comfortable for humans and demand good air circulation. Where summer temperatures will always remain above 50°, you can benefit your vandas by moving them outdoors during this period. Such a move should be made gradually to accustom the plant to the brighter outdoor light (see page 46).

V. coerulea. To 2 feet; large 3-4-inch flowers varying in color from pale to dark blue are produced from 1-2-foot stalks in late summer or fall. Strap leaves are 6-10 inches long.

V. sanderiana. To 3 feet; beautiful, flat 3-4-inch flowers in fall are a combination of white, rose, greenish yellow, brown, and dark red.

V. teres. To 7 feet; a terete-leafed species of great value in the tropical flower trade. Flowers are white and deep rose, 3-4 inches across, on stalks of 2-5 blooms in late spring and summer.

V. tricolor var. *suavis.* To 3 feet; sweetly fragrant flowers are white, spotted red-purple, to 3 inches across. Flowering season is winter.

EASILY-GROWN VANDA HYBRIDS, both strap-leaf sorts which are best for temperate conditions. V. x Rothschildiana (left) is blue; V. x Nellie Morley (right) is lavender-pink.

BASKETS of wire or slats with open spacing are necessary for stanhopeas to display their birdlike blooms; flower spikes grow down through potting mix, break through the bottom to flower.

Orchids in the Garden
Careful selection will take their beauty outdoors

GARDENERS in temperate parts of California and Florida and in all of Hawaii can use orchids as feature attractions in their landscapes. Some orchids will grow directly in the ground, others are better suited to containers where they can function as portable accent pieces. While cymbidiums, cattleyas, dendrobiums, and vandas are most often seen outdoors, there are a number of other attractive orchids described in this chapter that can provide color for your garden. In raised beds, you can have orchids as a spring or summer display in the same way you would use perennials or annuals. If you grow these orchids in containers you can continually shift new plants to display beds as they come into bloom.

In regions where summers are short, leave your orchids in their containers so they can be moved to shelter when the weather becomes unfavorable. In these cold areas, set plants outdoors from May through October. Hang pots or baskets from branches or place them strategically on the patio or terrace, but don't make the mistake of placing plants directly on trees; it takes almost a year for an orchid to become established on a branch, making this practice impossible in all but the mild winter climates.

If you do shift your tender orchids outdoors during the warm summer months, be sure to adjust them gradually to the outdoor atmosphere. See directions for this under "Orchids for the Patio" on page 47.

ORCHIDS IN THE GROUND

Orchid plants packaged in plastic are offered occasionally in supermarkets and nurseries; usually these will be bletillas, pleiones, or habenarias. Native wildflowers like cypripedium species and calypso are sometimes sold by specialty mail order houses. These, however, are generally difficult to transplant, so be prepared for a challenge if you try them.

Terrestrial orchids demand a well drained soil. Prepare beds by digging down at least 18 inches and replace the existing soil with a mix of equal parts garden loam and pulverized osmunda. A location which faces south or east is best although some species will bloom in a west-facing area, but cool and shaded north exposures should be avoided for all but the few (such as pleione and cypripedium) which require constant moisture combined with a cool atmosphere.

Orchids for Near-Tropical Regions

Gardeners in these continually warm and frequently moist areas have the greatest range of orchids from which to choose to decorate their gardens. Almost literally, the world is their greenhouse.

In southern Florida and in the Hawaiian Islands, local growers will offer a number of species and hybrids which you can grow outside in your garden. In tropical lands of Asia and the Americas, you may be able to collect (or to have collected) native orchids from nearby forests.

Orchids for Temperate Gardens

Which orchids are good risks for these gardens depends upon the definition of "temperate." Some of the orchids in the following list will survive temperatures down to freezing but not below it; others will take varying degrees of frost. Temperature tolerances are indicated for each genus described.

Bletilla. These orchids have the advantage of being readily available, inexpensive, and easy to grow. Lavender, cattleya-shaped, 1-2-inch flowers are produced up to a dozen on 18-24-inch stems. Leaves are grassy, pale green and plaited, from 3-6 to a plant. In fall, plant the tuberlike roots in a sandy soil where they will receive dappled sun or light shade and plenty of water during their growing season. After blooming, in early summer, let foliage ripen naturally; when the foliage begins to die back keep the plants barely moist until new growth starts in spring. Plants are hardy to about 20°; mulch them with straw in colder climates. Bletilla can be divided in early spring before growth starts, but don't do it too often; bloom is best when plants are crowded. *Bletilla striata*, sometimes sold as *B. hyacinthina*, is the species you will find available; occasionally a white-flowered variety is obtainable.

Calopogon pulchellus. This deciduous orchid is native to eastern North America in shaded to sunny bogs. From two to a dozen vibrant purple flowers, each characterized by a bearded lip, are produced in fall on 18-20-inch stems. Foliage is grassy, with only one leaf to each corm-like rhizome, but plants form large clumps of many leaves.

Calypso bulbosa. Here is another North American native which will withstand sub-zero temperatures. From each plant, less than a foot tall, comes a single, oval, dark green leaf. The pink flowers are solitary, pendant, an inch or more across with brown spots in lines, and purple and yellow markings in the pouchlike lip. Plant the corm-like rootstocks about 3 inches deep in leaf mold.

Cymbidium. Of all the orchids suitable for outdoor culture, cymbidiums are the most widely grown. These fine plants can reach 3-5 feet tall when flowering outdoors in all-year temperate climates—either in pots or in the ground. During the summer months especially, they need cool nights (from 45°-60°) to initiate flower buds, and they will require protection from slugs and snails. Cymbidiums will endure temperatures as low as 28° for a short time only; where harder frosts threaten, protect plants with a covering of polyethylene plastic. Flower spikes are more tender than are other plant tissues. For more information on cymbidiums, see pages 59-60.

HARDY TERRESTRIAL species Bletilla striata is readily available and easy to grow.

CYMBIDIUMS IN FLOWER are outstanding patio subjects in winter and spring. Here, containers are concealed by potted azaleas and cyclamen.

RELIABLE OUTDOOR PERFORMER in temperate climates is the cattleya-like Laeila anceps.

REED-STEM EPIDENDRUMS come in many bright colors, each flower shaped like small cattleya.

Cypripedium. Here you will find the lady's slippers and moccasin flowers—terrestrial orchids native to the northern hemisphere. Each flower with pouchlike lip appears well above the foliage on a slender, straight stem. All species prefer a neutral to slightly acid soil that is rich in organic matter and well drained. Planting location should be cool with filtered sun.

C. acaule (pink lady's slipper). Solitary rose-pink flowers appear in May and June above two oval, 6-9-inch long leaves that are flat to the ground. Cold winters and an acid, leafy soil are needed for it to thrive.

C. calceolus pubescens (yellow lady's slipper). Stems from 1-2 feet have yellow flowers with twisted sepals in May and June. This also needs cold winters to thrive.

C. californicum. Grows in boggy areas of northern California and southern Oregon where it blooms in summer with as many as a dozen flowers to a leafy stem. Sepals are small and greenish yellow to brown, petals are yellow, while the pouch is white to pink and spotted with brown.

C. reginae (showy lady's slipper). Another species that requires cold winters to grow well, this has white sepals and petals with a rose pink pouch. From 1 to 3 flowers to each stem appear in June. Plants grow 2-2½ feet tall.

Epidendrum. This genus includes epiphytic and terrestrial plants, most of which are easy to grow. Those with hard, round pseudobulbs and thick leathery leaves are sun and drought tolerant and need a rest period after flowering. The softer-textured plants with thin stemlike pseudobulbs do best with more shade and moisture throughout the year.

Reed-stemmed types need an abundance of sun to flower but require cool roots. Mulch plants growing in the ground to achieve a cool root area. Foliage will turn bright red and burn if the sun is too hot. On the other end of the scale, frost will burn tips at 28°, and plants will be killed to the ground at about 22°. In cold-winter areas grow the reed-stemmed types in pots and move them indoors in winter. All epidendrums will grow well in fir bark or other potting mixtures described on page 18. Those in bark will need to be fertilized at every other watering with a liquid fertilizer; plants in other mixtures will require fertilizer monthly. When blooms fade, cut the flowering stem back to within 1 or 2 joints of the ground.

E. cochleatum. This tropical American native has pear-shaped pseudobulbs 2-5 inches high with one or more leaves as long or longer. The erect flower stems bear 5-10 flowers, each 2-3 inches across. Flowers have narrow, twisted yellow-green sepals and petals, and a purplish black lip with lighter veins. Blooming season is irregular. Plants will withstand temperatures down to about 25°.

E. ibaguense (E. radicans). This species, from South America, produces erect, reedlike, leafy stems that will reach 2-4 feet. On slender stems that rise well above the foliage appear dense, globular clusters of 1-1½-inch orange-yellow flowers at various times throughout the year. Many hybrids are sold with flowers of other colors: yellow, pink, red, lavender, and white.

E. o'brienianum. This is the best known of the reed-stem types. Dense clusters of vivid red flowers—each the shape of a miniature cattleya—are carried on slender stems 1-2 feet above the foliage.

Epipactis. The stream orchis (*E. gigantea*) is found growing near streams in many parts of the western United States—including some of the coldest climates. Lance-shaped leaves to 8 inches long grow from creeping rootstocks, from which arise 1-3-foot flower stems in summer. The 1-inch flowers, 3-10 to each stalk, are green veined with purple. Grows easily in a rich, moist soil in sun or partial shade. Plants are divided in fall.

Habenaria. A large group of temperate and tropical orchids, some of these may be grown outdoors without risk in the coldest gardening climates. Let the native location of any species be your guide to hardiness. The most frequently sold species—*H. radiata*, the egret flower—is from Japan and will endure temperatures to the low 20's only. The egret flower carries from 3-5 1-inch flowers on slender, leafy stems that may reach 2 feet above a rosette of strap-shaped leaves. Sepals and a trailing spur are green, petals are white—one of which flares to 1 inch wide with fringed edges like feathers on the wing of a bird in flight. A soil that is composed of leaf mold or of equal parts peat moss, sand, and good garden soil will suit these plants provided you never let them dry out.

Laelia. Several species are well-suited to outdoor culture where temperatures seldom dip below freezing; if winter readings are likely to go down

FRAGRANT MEXICAN NATIVE,
Laelia albida, *displays its white,
lavender, and yellow flowers
outdoors in late winter where
temperatures are moderate.*

to the mid-30's, grow these in the most frost-protected garden areas. Cattleya-type flowers are produced on long arching stems, the successive blooms stretching the blooming period to a month or more. Plants also resemble cattleyas. Grow in filtered shade, either in pots or on slabs of fern or bark; potting material (bark or osmunda) should dry out between waterings.

L. albida. Fragrant 2-inch flowers are transparent white with a yellow rib in the throat and a lavender flush on the lip, appearing in winter. Species is rare in collections.

L. anceps. Flowers are rose-violet with purple-lined yellow throat, 4 inches across, 2-6 on each stem in fall and winter.

L. autumnalis. Fragrant, rose-purple, 4-inch flowers appear in fall, 3-9 on each erect stem.

Pleione. These orchids are as easy to grow as ordinary spring bulb plants. Plants have angular pseudobulbs topped with a few folded leaves, usually deciduous after the flowering period. Flowers are 3-4 inches, one to a stem. Most species are hardy to about 10°, but blossoms of winter flowering species may need protection where temperatures go much below freezing.

After flowering, separate the clumps of pseudobulbs and plant them in a mixture of leaf mold, chopped osmunda and sphagnum, and sand. Until the roots are actively growing and growth begins, be careful not to give them too much water. Once growth is underway, however, plants should receive generous amounts of water. When new pseudobulbs are mature (this is when the leaf is extended), withhold water for several weeks to encourage formation of flower buds.

Pleione humilis (white, with yellow and violet on lip), P. maculata (white and purple), and P. praecox (red-purple) are winter flowering; P. formosana (lavender-purple with brown and yellow on lip) blooms in spring.

Orchids for Cold Winter Regions

If winter temperatures are likely to drop to 20° or lower for any extended periods, you can assume you have a cold winter climate for orchids. There are some species described in the preceding section of "Orchids for temperate gardens" which will endure your cold weather, but your choice is more limited. Any of the following orchids might be grown outside the year around through all but possibly the most extreme winters: Calopogon pulchellus; Calypso bulbosa; Cypripedium acaule, C. pubescens, C. reginae; pleione species.

LIVE OAK TRUNK supports vigorous growth of Laelia anceps in the Sunset garden. Flowering begins in late fall.

EASTER ORCHID, Pleione formosana, resembles a small, fringed-lip cattleya in traditional orchid color: lavender-pink. Flowers appear in early spring, sometimes before leaves.

FAVORED OUTDOOR CONDITIONS are present in this patio: ventilation, humidity, and filtered sun.

LAZY-SUSAN plant stand for temperate gardens will accommodate many orchids in small space.

HAWAIIAN LANDSCAPE features dendrobiums growing in containers alongside a garden path.

ORCHIDS FOR THE PATIO

Most orchids are tropical in appearance and will lend an exotic air to your terrace or patio. Species and hybrids that bloom during spring and summer will, of course, be enjoyed the most during the outdoor-living months.

Before setting plants outdoors, prepare them for brighter light than they are accustomed to receiving inside. To do this, first put them in a somewhat shady place, then move them to dappled sunlight for a few days, and finally shift them into direct sun. Observe leaves to be sure they are not being scorched from too much sun. Plants will appreciate frequent sprayings with water, as long as this moisture is gone by dusk.

The following orchids, suitable for growing outdoors during the months when temperatures remain above 50°, will provide you with colorful flowers at that time (see pages 31-38 for descriptions).

Aerides species

Ansellia africana

Brassia maculata

Cattleya hybrids

Dendrobium chrysotoxum

D. densiflorum

D. farmeri

D. pierardii

Epidendrum species and hybrids

Miltonia hybrids

Odontoglossum grande

Oncidium sarcodes

Vanda teres

V. tricolor var. *suavis*

Outdoors, orchid plants benefit greatly from natural air currents and rain, but you should attempt to keep plants evenly moist. During sunny weather you may have to water them daily because the free flowing air outdoors will evaporate moisture quickly. The best type of location for orchids is a sheltered area where there is some sunlight. Since orchids like bottom ventilation, potted plants used outdoors should not be placed directly on the ground or patio floor. You can easily make platforms of redwood laths for your container-grown orchids or place the pots on bricks spaced an inch or more apart.

MOST POPULAR outdoor orchid for western gardens is the cymbidium; bloom is in winter, spring.

Increasing Your Collection

Divisions, seedlings, and imported plants

AFTER you have grown a few orchids, you will find that you want more. It is impossible to resist their beauty. But before you begin to buy additional plants you would be wise to plan your purchases. By so doing you will ultimately derive the greatest possible satisfaction for the money spent while keeping disappointments to a minimum.

Of the two "rules" which you should consider when purchasing new orchids, the first is to buy only plants that will thrive in the conditions you can offer them. If you have a warm growing area, concentrate on such kinds as cattleyas, epidendrums, some dendrobiums, and ansellias. If the area is cool, select miltonias, odontoglossums, some oncidiums, and zygopetalums. Read the descriptions of these and other orchids on pages 31-38 to determine the plants' temperature tolerances.

The second "rule" to remember in any orchid purchase is to buy the best possible plants you can afford. This means that you should avoid both unhealthy bargain plants and those which bear inferior flowers for their type. Look for plants with healthy green growth and fresh white-tipped roots; these will be in prime shape to easily adjust to a new environment in your home. Healthy mature plants will give you the most enjoyment in the least amount of time. Especially to the new orchid grower who would like to see flowers during the first year, mature plants are worth the slightly greater expense.

WHERE TO BUY PLANTS

There are two kinds of orchid nurseries: those that sell commercial cut flowers and retail plants as a sideline, and those that specialize only in the sale of plants. In most cut flower orchid nurseries there will be counters of plants for sale which, although desirable for the hobbyist, are not up to standards set for commercial cut blooms. These plants are mature specimens and are usually a good buy. Avoid the bargain counters of plants that have been heavily fertilized to produce many flowers. These plants are often exhausted from this forced flower production and may require two or three years to regain their normal vigor and produce typical blooms.

The nursery that specializes in plants alone is likely to have a larger selection of plants than will the cut flower establishments. This grower is usually interested in your problems and is

HOW TO IMPORT ORCHIDS

Many orchid growers, after having successfully grown hybrid plants, decide they would like to try some species orchids collected from their native habitats. These are not the sorts that usually win blue ribbons at orchid shows, but they invariably have a wild charm that makes worthwhile the extra initial effort necessary for reestablishing them in captivity.

To import wild orchids, you first must get lists from collectors, study them, and decide what plants you'd like to have. Then, write to the United States Department of Agriculture, Plant Quarantine Division, 209 River Street, Hoboken, New Jersey 07030, and ask for a permit to import orchids. You will receive with your permit detailed instructions regarding your responsibilities and those of the shipper.

Plants sent by air mail or air parcel post arrive the most quickly, and you will not need to deal with the United States Customs. Any customs duties on small shipments will be handled at your post office. Your plants will be inspected at the point of entry to this country, fumigated or treated with insecticide, and shipped on to you under the original postage provided.

After opening your shipment, carefully remove plants and air them to dissipate any fumigant residue. Then follow the steps illustrated below.

Careful watering is necessary with collected orchids; they may have few or no live roots, and as a result will not be able to use heavy applications of water.

1. Open package immediately upon arrival to let any residual fumigant disperse.

2. Inspect plants and remove any badly damaged, decayed, or crushed portions of roots and leaves.

3. Make solution of ¾ cup sugar to 1 gallon water. Clean leaves with it, dip roots for 1 hour.

4. To revive dried plants, wrap in damp newspaper, let plants sit overnight to regain moisture.

ORCHID NURSERIES offer a bewildering array of plants, can even ship them in bloom.

BACK BULBS may produce new plants from dormant eyes when potted in bark, sand, or vermiculite.

willing to give advice to make you a satisfied customer. He will be able to tell you if the orchid you want is fresh from the jungle and not yet established, and will, in such cases, probably suggest that you purchase something else.

See page 64 for more orchid shopping ideas.

NEW PLANTS FROM OLD

Most orchids with a sympodial growth habit (see page 10) can be divided, as you might divide bulbs, to produce more plants of the same kind. Select a strong plant with 8 or more pseudobulbs or stems which has grown too large for its container. Divide the plant by severing with a sharp sterile knife the rhizome at the point where the cut will leave 4 pseudobulbs or stems to each division. Then carefully pull apart the mass of roots. Such a strong division will establish itself so rapidly that blossoms may be borne on the next year's growth.

Don't throw away orchid stems or old "back bulbs" (those pseudobulbs, taken from the rear of the plant, that no longer bear leaves); many times they can be induced to grow new shoots by placing them partially buried in damp sand or vermiculite in a warm place. Be sure to leave the growing eye or bud (at the base of the pseudobulb, or at the nodes on stems) exposed to the air. Plants produced from back bulbs or stems generally require 3 to 5 years to mature.

Monopodial orchids (those that grow vertically rather than horizontally) can also be propagated by the amateur orchid grower. However, a number of years is needed to produce mature plants, and danger to the parent plant is often high since, in many cases, removal of the growing tip is necessary to stimulate production of offshoots which are later removed to develop into new plants. If you want to have more plants of vanda, phalaenopsis, and others of this growth habit you should buy either mature specimens or healthy seedlings of any size.

Meristem culture is a specialized method of rapidly increasing individual plants, especially those of a scarce new hybrid. From the plant's growing tip, the embryonic growth cell is removed and cultured in a nutrient solution where it reproduces itself many times. Later, these cells are separated into individual flasks in which they grow into seedling-sized plants identical to that from which the original growth cell was taken. Hybrids reproduced in this manner may be designated "mericlones."

OFFSHOOTS (kikis) are produced on stems or from bases of many orchids, will form new plants.

DETACHED OFFSHOOT with good root and stem development is ready to be planted on its own.

OVERGROWN CATTLEYA (shown on page 18) is easily divided with sterilized clippers or knife. Make cuts in the old rhizome so that each new division will have 4 pseudobulbs.

SEEDLING CULTURE

Growing orchids from seed is a time consuming process best left to experienced specialists. However, you can buy flasks of small seedling plants ready to be transferred to community pots. You will ultimately have the pleasure of seeing your own unique seedlings produce their first flowers, but without having to be involved with the laboratory procedures needed for germinating the seeds.

Many orchid suppliers offer flasks of seedlings which contain about 200 tiny plants. These plantlets are ready to come out of the flask when they are about 1/2 inch high; usually they are at this size when you buy them.

ORCHID SEEDLINGS begin their lives in flasks of sterilized agar with nutrients for growth.

Some commercial orchid growers offer a "custom seeding service" which is an advantage to amateur orchid enthusiasts who want to raise seedlings from particular parent plants but who lack the facilities to germinate the seeds. For an established fee, the grower will germinate the seeds from the seed capsule which you take to him; you get the seedling plants when they are large enough to be removed from the seedling flasks to a community pot.

The Community Pot

Before removing seedlings from their flask for potting, you should assemble all the materials you will need for the operation. A number of 3-5 inch pots (well-scrubbed and dipped in boiling water, if they have been used before) should be soaked in water for several hours so that they will not extract any water from the orchid compost. When this is completed and the pots are ready for use, fill the pots one-third full with clean pieces of broken pottery and then add a potting mixture composed of equal parts chopped tree fern fiber, ground fir bark, and osmunda. Pack the mix tightly into the pot and water it.

Planting the seedlings is the easiest part of the operation. Punch small holes in the potting mixture with the tip of a pencil and set the tiny plants in place. About 20-30 plants can be accommodated in a community pot.

Spring is the best time of year for moving seedlings. This gives them the greatest possible amount of time to grow before any dormant period in fall or winter.

Seedlings in their first community pot require a humid location and a relatively constant temperature in the 67°-80° range. A greenhouse satisfies their needs easily. Lacking this, the home orchid grower can buy or easily make a small glass case to house the pots of seedlings. Even a packing box with a glass pane over the top may be suitable. Whatever you use, the seedlings should be placed in a bright but not sunny spot.

Never allow the potting mixture to dry out, but remember that a soggy condition is just as unsatisfactory. Once-a-day watering will probably be necessary, but this should be done early enough so that foliage will be dry before twilight to avoid encouraging diseases. On sunny days the seedlings will benefit from a fine misting during the day, but early enough so that leaves can dry before dusk. Open the seedlings' enclo-

VANDA SEEDLINGS before their first bloom: those in hanging pots are old enough to flower; plants in small pots will need one more transplanting.

sure for an hour or two each day to allow air to circulate in and around the plants.

Transplanting Seedlings

It will be about a year (depending upon the orchid species grown) before the seedlings are ready for transplanting. For this second move, put 5 or 6 plants into a clean 3-inch pot in the same type compost. Give them more light and some weak fertilizer once a month.

In another year or so, when the plants start to crowd one another, they are ready for individual pots. Transplant them into small grade fir bark or into osmunda in 2 or 3-inch containers.

A final transplanting is necessary, after about one more year, at which time they should go into individual 5-inch pots in medium grade fir bark. Most plants will flower in these pots.

If the above procedure seems lengthy to you, buy orchids in the 2 or 3-inch pot stage. Plants will be sturdy and will have passed the most crucial time of their lives; they will be about 3 years old (from seed), ready for their third transplanting. Depending on the vigor of the plants, a fourth potting will bring them up to blooming size.

AFTER SECOND TRANSPLANT, 3-6 orchid seedlings will be large enough for planting together.

Utilizing Orchid Flowers

Distinctive decorations with superlative lasting qualities

ALTHOUGH suggesting the use of orchids as cut flowers in the home may sound extravagant, it is really quite practical: Most orchid flowers will last for a month or more in water. Any other cut flowers would have to be replaced several times with fresh material in that span of time. Not only are orchids long-lasting—they are also highly individualistic blossoms, able to attract attention wherever you might use them.

Orchid corsages are another fringe-benefit available to the home orchid grower. The skill of a florist is not required for you to produce a professional-appearing product.

With both arrangements in the home and corsages for special occasions, you will have the additional satisfaction of having grown the orchids yourself. As few as a dozen plants, selected for differing seasons of bloom, can furnish flowers almost all year.

ARRANGEMENTS WITH ORCHIDS

Although nearly all orchids may be cut for decorative purposes, there are several types that, because of better lasting qualities or superior flowers, stand out above all others as first-rate cut flowers. Many of the oncidiums, with hundreds of 1/2-inch flowers in branched sprays of blossoms, will stay fresh in a vase of water for 6 or 7 weeks. Most flowers in this group are bright yellow, usually marked with chocolate brown. These sprays of flowers are usually most effective by themselves against a light-colored background. Portions of the flower sprays can be incorporated in arrangements of other small flowers such as stock and snapdragons.

Lycastes come in many colors, but the larger-flowered types are generally pink or apple green. These blooms will hold color in water for a month, sometimes longer if the arrangement is in a cool location. The size and dramatic nature of these flowers combined with their heavy texture calls for using them by themselves. They do not blend well with other flowers.

The majority of cattleyas have large blossoms, 4 inches or more across, and are best used for corsages. Their short stems make them more difficult to utilize in arrangements, although you can float cattleyas in a bowl of water just as you might camellias or gardenias.

The excellent lasting quality of cymbidiums perfectly suits them for use as cut flowers but, as with cattleyas, the individual flower stems are too short for arrangements. Their long spikes

DELICATE, almost feathery
epidendrums need no additional
material to create a lovely
and effective arrangement.

with many open flowers, however, are easy to work into graceful compositions where they might be displayed only with complementary foliage.

Paphiopedilum species and hybrids have several qualities which mark them as excellent cut flower subjects. Long wiry stems make it easy for you to arrange the flowers, while their often exotic colors, intricate patterns, and lacquer-like texture insure that they will not be overlooked.

The moth orchid (phalaenopsis) now has hybrids with pink or yellow flowers in addition to the familiar white. They are carried on long, arching stems—resembling a flight of some beautiful tropical insect. Cut the entire stem for a handsome floral piece, or float single blooms in a bowl of water. Phalaenopsis as a cut flower does not last as long as the other orchids just described—3 weeks is the usual life-span.

Because of their unique flower structure, orchids are best appreciated in arrangements that are of simple design. Strive for simplicity of line and form, which will give emphasis to the beauty, texture, and color of individual flowers. Mass displays of orchid flowers are often more overpowering than they are beautiful. Cutting the flowers never harms the plants, but never cut orchid foliage.

DRIFTWOOD AND EVERGREEN needles are perfect color companions for paphiopedilum flowers.

CORSAGES

Because of their long lasting-qualities, orchids are superior corsage flowers. Almost any orchid can be used for this purpose, and having them growing in your home is a convenience when you need corsages for festive occasions. The flowers are so lovely that cutting them from the plant will take courage at first, but as your collection grows the temptation to use your own flowers will win out.

So that the flowers will have their full color, cut them after they have been open on the plant for a few days. Use a sterile razor blade when cutting the flower stems. Then cut a thin, angled slice from the end of the stem. This allows the stem to take up water more readily than does a cut made directly across the stem.

In corsages of single flowers the orchid should be worn right side up—as it naturally grows. When corsages contain several flowers, at least one (and preferably the dominant flower) should be in its natural position.

Ribbon bows are effective complements to orchid blooms, but use ribbon sparingly to avoid detracting from the flowers. In pinning a corsage to clothing, secure the pin through the ribbon—not through the stem.

While it is being worn, the stem of the flower can be inserted in a glass vial of water to keep it fresh. Vials for this purpose (available from florist suppliers) have a rubber cap with a hole through which you insert the stem for its entire length. If you cannot locate glass vials, you can encase the stem in moist cotton which then should be wrapped in plastic. For better appearance the plastic-wrapped cotton can be covered with floral tape.

When the corsage is not being worn, put the flowers in the refrigerator where the temperature will not be lower than 45°F. A refrigerator's vegetable compartment will usually provide the proper conditions. Stems can be left in the glass vial or moistened cotton. Placed on a bed of shredded wax paper in a polyethylene plastic bag, orchid flowers will remain fresh for many days if the opening of the bag is securely folded shut.

1. Cut orchid flower, leaving 1-1½ inches of stem; insert florist wire through stem near flower.

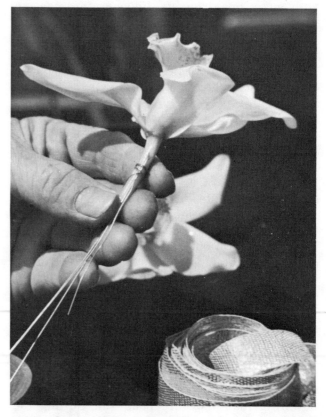

2. Bend wire down alongside each side of stem; take second wire and wrap around stem in spiral.

3. Using green floral tape, securely wrap the stem and first few inches of wire extending beyond.

4. For a multiple-flowered corsage, wrap several wired flowers together with floral tape.

5. For an easy "bow", form several loops of ribbon, gather together at center, tie with wire.

6. Attach wired ribbon to the wired flower stems. wrap with floral tape for finished corsage.

Specialties

Four orchids favored throughout the world

THERE are many kinds of orchids, strikingly different in appearance from one another, yet through the years certain ones have emerged as the most popular. Colorful, large-flowered cattleyas, exotic cypriprediums, the etherial phalaenopsis, and floriferous cymbidiums lead the way in the orchid world's parade of favorites. None of these are difficult plants to grow and most of them will reward the grower with a bountiful harvest of flowers. The number of named hybrids runs into the thousands, indicating the popularity of these four enticing orchid types.

CATTLEYAS

Today, after years of extensive hybridizing, cattleya hybrids may be found in all colors except blue and black. The bronze or orange-shaded hybrids and the brilliant reds, for example, are startlingly different from the traditional lavender cattleyas employed for so many years as corsage flowers and from which the color "orchid" was named. In addition to new colors, the hybridizers have produced plants whose bloom seasons will collectively cover the entire year; a selection of only 6 cattleyas could give you some color in all seasons. Mature plants are available at moderate prices, these depending upon the hybrid's color, the size of flowers it bears, and the size of the plant.

Cattleyas are sun lovers, so a western or southern exposure suits them well. Plants will grow at other exposures, but bloom will be sparse.

Pot your cattleyas either in osmunda or in fir bark (see page 18); the latter is especially good for encouraging root growth in young plants. Because bloom tends to be more abundant when roots are confined, use relatively small pots when you plant your cattleyas.

Ideal temperatures for cattleyas correspond to average home conditions — 55°-62° at night and fifteen degrees warmer by day. Plants will survive lower or higher temperatures but will not bloom abundantly. At lower temperatures growth is slow, and at higher temperatures growth is too rapid and plants become depleted. Most problems with cattleyas come with hot weather rather than with coolness. Plants can tolerate as much as 95° for a few hours, but on very hot days be sure to mist plants frequently to lower the temperature. At the same time keep the growing area well ventilated (see page 16).

TYPICAL of modern cattleya hybrids, with broad, heavily fringed petals and lip, is Laeliocattleya Fred B. Castator 'Caballero'.

Success with cattleyas depends largely upon watering practices. These plants like to dry out thoroughly between waterings. However, this doesn't mean they do not like moisture. In summer, when the transpiration rate is high, they need copious watering. In winter, keep plants just barely moist but not so dry that the pseudobulbs shrivel. Always flood pots until excess water runs out the bottom.

To determine when to water plants, feel the osmunda fiber or force your fingers between the pot and the fir bark. If the potting material is springy and cool to the touch, it still holds enough water; if it is crisp and woody it needs watering again. Fir bark lets water run through quickly; osmunda, on the other hand, holds water well and stays moist longer than bark. Plants in bark, therefore, will always need more frequent watering than will plants in osmunda.

In osmunda, plants need fertilizer only occasionally because the fibers contain some nutrients. Once a month in summer and not at all during the rest of the year is sufficient for the osmunda-grown plant. In fir bark, which is nearly devoid of nutrients, fertilizing may be done about twice a month during spring and summer and once a month in fall. Do not feed plants in winter when light intensity is low and plant growth is naturally slow.

CYMBIDIUMS

Graceful plants lavish with bloom, cymbidiums are favorites in the home and the garden wherever nighttime temperatures fall to 60° or lower during the warmest months of the year. From long, narrow, arching foliage arise erect or arching spikes of flowers, usually from February to early May. One spike may carry as many as 30 flowers, each 4-5 inches across, which can remain fresh and attractive for eight or more weeks. Robust, mature plants may reach 3-5 feet high when in full bloom.

Most cymbidium growers list only hybrids in their catalogs—large-flowered varieties with white, pink, yellow, green, or bronze blooms, which usually have yellow throats and dark red markings on the lip. Where space is limited— either indoors or outside—the miniature cymbidium hybrids will give you the same beauty at about one-fourth the size.

Today, most cymbidiums are hybrids of cool growing types, and although they will tolerate

HYBRID CYMBIDIUM Green Jade has smooth color in sepals and petals, precise lip markings.

BOUNTIFUL DISPLAY of blooms is produced by mature specimen of cymbidium hybrid Jade.

heat if necessary, they must have cool night temperatures (45°-55°) throughout the summer and early fall to set flower buds. Miniature cymbidiums will tolerate more heat than the large standard sorts, but they still prefer cool conditions.

From March to October—the months in which new growth develops and matures—water plants copiously. At other times, keep the potting mix barely moist but never dry.

Many composts are available for cymbidiums, from osmunda to fir bark to various mixtures of these and other organic materials. A good potting mixture for cymbidiums is 2 parts redwood bark, 2 parts peat moss, and 1 part sand. Another popular mix contains 2 parts each of fir bark, leaf mold, peat moss, and 1 part sand. Packaged mixes specifically for cymbidiums are very satisfactory, and the easiest approach if you have never grown these orchids. Whatever mixture you use, it should drain fast yet retain moisture.

Cymbidiums need additional fertilizers. Give them a complete liquid fertilizer every two weeks from January through July; fertilize about once a month from August through December.

Do not disturb plants too often, because most cymbidiums bloom better when pot-bound. Repot them after blooming but only when the pseudobulbs become crowded against the edges of their containers. Water lightly after repotting; when new growth is evident, increase moisture.

When you divide cymbidiums, keep a minimum of 3 healthy pseudobulbs (with foliage) in each division. Dust cuts with sulfur or paint them with tree seal to discourage rot.

PAPHIOPEDILUMS
(Cypripediums)

The lovely lady's slipper orchids—species and hybrids of paphiopedilum, cypripedium, or phragmipedium—bear flowers in striking, often bizarre, color combinations: white, yellow, green with white stripes, pure green, or a combination of background colors and markings in tan, mahogany brown, maroon, green, and white. With their lacquered or waxy textures, they sometimes appear more artificial than real. You will almost always find them sold as cypripediums, but the vast majority of plants in commerce are species or hybrids of paphiopedilum, originally from tropical regions of Asia. True cypripediums are native to temperate regions of the northern hemisphere (see page 43).

Paphiopedilum foliage is either grassy green or mottled. Usually the plain-leafed forms flower in winter, the mottled-leaf forms flower in summer, although some will bloom on and off throughout the year. A robust, mature plant can bear as many as 30 flowers at once.

Some paphiopedilums are found high in the mountains where it is cool and moist, others dwell on warm forest floors; because of these differences in native habitats, two kinds of culture are necessary. Green-leafed paphiopedilums are cool growing and require a night temperature of 50°-55° and about 70° during the day. In hot summer weather, try to keep heat down by misting plants. Warm growing species, recognized by their mottled foliage, need about 60°-65° at night and from 70°-85° during the day. They will tolerate more heat in summer than the green-leafed types.

Unlike cattleyas that require almost full sun, paphiopedilums do best in dappled to bright light without direct sunshine. Extreme sun will scorch leaves and quickly desiccate plants. Grow them at south or west windows or, if necessary, even at a north exposure, but always away from direct exposure to sun. Avoid an east-facing location for them.

Growth is continuous in these orchids, and they have no pseudobulbs to store moisture to tide them over during a dry spell, so keep the potting medium evenly moist all year. As with all orchids, water plants thoroughly until excess water runs out of the bottom of the container. This will flush out any salts that might otherwise accumulate and injure the roots.

Although paphiopedilums are basically terrestrial, they can be grown in equal parts of shredded osmunda and garden loam or in medium grade fir bark. Repot plants yearly after bloom; if large, divide them keeping three growths to a container. Do not pot paphiopedilums as tightly as you would cattleyas, but be sure the potting mix is well settled in the pot. After repotting, water plants only enough to keep the compost barely moist. When new growth begins (in about three weeks) regular watering can be started. Do

HYBRID PAPHIOPEDILUMS display variation in both form and color. P. Rosy Dawn (left) is white with pink to maroon dots; P. Sandra Mary (right) is rose, brown, and white.

PAPHIOPEDILUM HYBRIDS reflect the efforts of orchid breeders. These have broader flower parts, smoother and clearer colors than many species (see page 7).

not allow water to remain in leaf axils or you may encourage the growth of a bacterial rot.

Give paphiopedilum plants a moderate amount of moisture in the air (30-50 per cent humidity) and maintain the good air circulation that virtually all orchids require (see page 16). Paphiopedilum roots are extremely sensitive to fertilizers, so any applications should be weaker than the directions specify. If you grow them in fir bark, weak applications of fertilizer may be necessary throughout spring and summer.

PHALAENOPSIS

The name "moth orchid" gives you an idea of the delicacy and grace which characterize phalaenopsis flowers and the manner in which they are carried on their stems. The sight of six to a dozen white flowers on a gracefully arching stem suggests a swarm of moths or butterflies in flight. White-flowered species and hybrids, closely followed by pink sorts, have been the most widely grown colors, but yellow and multicolored hybrids are now available with the same refinement and delicacy of the traditional white sorts. Indi-

vidual flowers last for two months or more, and the succession of blooms from one plant may give you flowers for more than half the year.

Phalaenopsis orchids are native to the tropics of Asia, extending as far west as Africa and south to Australia. Their preferred temperature range—around 65° at night and 10-15 degrees warmer during the day—is a very comfortable household environment. What the ordinary home does not supply, without special attention, is the preferred humidity; 60-70 per cent humidity makes orchids comfortable but not the humans who live with them. A greenhouse most easily provides the *ideal* humidity; see page 14 for ways to increase humidity around orchids grown in the home.

Phalaenopsis is a relatively shade-loving genus, most happy with about half the amount of light required by cattleyas. Although they can tolerate more light during fall and winter than during the summer months, they must not be subjected to direct sunlight.

Either fir bark or osmunda is a suitable potting material for phalaenopsis plants; see page 18 for potting techniques. Phalaenopsis differs from many other commonly-grown orchids, however, by its infrequent need for repotting. Growth habit is *monopodial* (see page 10), which allows you to leave a plant undisturbed in its container until the potting mixture begins to break down and lose its open texture.

When you repot a phalaenopsis, first prepare your potting material and container as described on page 18. Then, remove the plant from the container in which it is growing and clean off all old potting mixture. You will see that the plant consists of a stem, topped by the leaves, which has a live but inactive stub with remains of dead roots. Above this stub will be a ring of living roots. Break off the inactive stub below the living roots (or cut it off with a sterilized knife) and position the plant in the new container so that the base of the leaves will be even with the surface of the potting mixture. Trim live roots only to whatever extent is needed to fit them into the pot. Potting mixture should be firmed around roots, but not as tightly as for cattleyas. Following the spring bloom or when new roots are forming are the best times to repot a phalaenopsis.

Because they have no pseudobulbs in which to store moisture, phalaenopsis plants must never be allowed to dry out completely. They are no exception, however, in requiring good drainage and aeration, so that you must be careful not to overwater. See page 21 for watering guidelines.

Especially during periods of active growth, phalaenopsis plants appreciate applications of liquid fertilizer with every other watering. In the less active growing seasons it is best not to fertilize.

The monopodial growth habit of phalaenopsis makes it impractical for the home orchid grower to try to produce additional plants from the ones in his collection. Seeding phalaenopsis plants, however, grow so rapidly that they usually reach flowering size within three years. If you wish to have additional plants at the least possible expense, buy a flask of seedlings ready to be transferred to community pots and follow the procedures outlined on pages 52-53. Repotting will be necessary about every six months—sometimes sooner if the seedlings become too large for the pots in less time.

WHITE PHALAENOPSIS *flowers embody all the grace and lightness which earned for them the name "moth orchid." The hybrid at right, Fairway Park, shows the intricate lip structure.*

INDEX

Boldface numbers refer to photographs

SHOPPING FOR ORCHIDS